WE MAKE A LIFE BY WHAT WE GIVE

Philanthropic and Nonprofit Studies

Dwight F. Burlingame and David C. Hammack, editors

WE MAKE A LIFE BY WHAT WE GIVE

Richard B. Gunderman

Indiana University Press
Bloomington and Indianapolis

This book is a publication of

Indiana University Press
601 North Morton Street
Bloomington, Indiana 47404-3797 USA

www.iupress.indiana.edu

Telephone orders	800-842-6796
Fax orders	812-855-7931
Orders by e-mail	iuporder@indiana.edu

First paperback edition 2009
© 2008 by Richard B. Gunderman
All rights reserved

Manufactured in the United States of America

The Library of Congress has cataloged the hardcover edition as follows:

Gunderman, Richard B.
We make a life by what we give / Richard B. Gunderman.
p. cm. — (Philanthropic and nonprofit studies)
Includes bibliographical references and index.
ISBN-13: 978-0-253-35076-3 (cloth : alk. paper) 1. Generosity. 2. Sharing. 3. Altruism. I. Title.
BJ1533.G4G85 2008
177'.7—dc22

2007039605

ISBN: 978-0-253-20029-7 (pbk.)

1 2 3 4 5 14 13 12 11 10 09

CONTENTS

PREFACE

One of our first moral opportunities in life is to share. It is a lesson that we begin learning when we are very young, yet we cannot excel at as youngsters. Although children inspire us with beautiful acts of spontaneous generosity, they cannot grasp the full range of human needs and aspirations that inspire giving. As mature adults, we want to give richly and well. We aim not to extract from others as much as we can, but to contribute, to make a difference in their lives by giving the best of ourselves. To excel at it, we need to understand fully what it means to give. This book is about giving, and the ways in which it deepens and enriches human life.

There is no field of human endeavor that does not illustrate the importance of giving. As a physician, I am especially familiar with medicine, so I have drawn again and again on illustrations from the field of medicine. Each of us is both patient and caregiver, making the intersection of medicine and giving a particularly accessible territory to explore. We want to understand not only what it means to provide first-rate patient care but also genuinely to care for patients. By looking at giving through the eyes of our most astute thinkers and poets, we can become better doctors and more compassionate human beings.

Giving our best is not primarily a matter of managing money, nor is it about implementing a particular set of rules or moral principles. Giving well is about fully engaging our moral imaginations in the quest for a richer human life. It requires that we think and feel for ourselves, though not by ourselves. What follows is a series of essays that serve as invitations to ongoing dialogue on this vital topic. Because no discipline—not philosophy, religion, literature, biology, economics, history, or any other—holds a monopoly on giving, this is an inherently interdisciplinary inquiry. In the largest sense, it is about philanthropy, but of course calling it philanthropy raises as many questions as it answers.

ACKNOWLEDGMENTS

It is at least ironic and perhaps even inappropriate that a book on giving and gratitude should contain a section entitled "acknowledgments," when what is clearly called for is not acknowledgment but hearty thanks. The lenses through which this book explores giving were the gifts of many people, and were polished by still more. I hope they will find here recognizable traces of their own insights, for the text itself is the best thanks I can offer. In particular, I would like to thank Lenore Ealy, Dwight Burlingame, Leslie Lenkowsky, and Eugene Tempel for inviting me to participate in a variety of engaging philanthropic programs; Robert Payton, Paul Nagy, William Enright, Nancy Goldfarb, and Richard Klopp for years of delightful philanthropic conversation; the graduate and undergraduate students in the Department of Philosophy and the Center on Philanthropy at Indiana University, who have explored these ideas with me in classes and seminars; my parents, James and Marilyn Gunderman; and above all, my dear wife, Laura, and our wonderful children, Rebecca, Peter, David, and John.

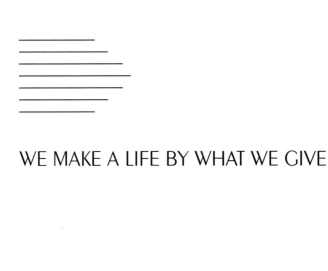

WE MAKE A LIFE BY WHAT WE GIVE

1

IMAGINING PHILANTHROPY

What is our image of philanthropy? This question is worth pondering because our philanthropic practice is powerfully informed by our philanthropic aspirations. A rich image can open up possibilities for philanthropic excellence, enhancing the lives of both givers and recipients. By contrast, defective images tend to promote poor philanthropic strategies—strategies that, far from enriching human lives, may actually impoverish them. No one pretends that the perfect image of philanthropy ever lies ready at hand. Philanthropy must grow, develop, and adapt along with the changing human context in which it is embedded. Yet bringing it to fullest fruition in our own place and time is an essential mission for each generation.

What kind of philanthropy can we imagine? The answer depends in part on what we understand philanthropy to be. The very meaning of the term is open to question.

- Does philanthropy refer strictly to large transfers of wealth? Or may giving take other equally legitimate forms, such as gifts of time and talent?
- Who does it? Is philanthropy strictly the province of non-profit foundations and their agents? Or is it also accessible to non-professionals?
- Who are its targets? Is philanthropy always directed to the public good? Or can it focus on private individuals as well?
- Does motive matter? Can we use taxes or shame to compel giving? Or must we give spontaneously of our own free will?
- Who benefits? Should philanthropic activity be devoted solely to the interests of the beneficiary? Or is there an opportunity to consider the welfare of the donor?
- How do we measure philanthropic performance? Is the ultimate criterion the monetary value of each bequest? Or do important aspects of philanthropy resist appraisal in dollars and cents?

By addressing these questions, we can challenge and stimulate our imagination as people committed to giving.

Context

How we answer such defining philanthropic questions hinges on the contexts in which we pose them. In philanthropy, as in every field of life, context always exerts an immense influence on the meaning of ideas. Consider each of the following riddles.

- I live above a star, and yet never burn
  I have eleven neighbors, and yet none of them turn
  I am visited in sequence, first, last, or in between
  PRS are my initials, now tell me what I mean
- A beggar's brother died, but the man who died had no brother. How can this be?
- What English word is most frequently pronounced incorrectly?

Each of these verbal puzzles represents an instance of what perceptual psychologists call a figure-ground problem. Our visual assessment of a figure's size, hue, shape, and motion depend in large part on the background against which it is projected. Simply by changing the background, we can make the large appear small, the dark appear light, the straight appear curved, and the static appear moving.

Before we can solve such verbal puzzles, we need to examine carefully the mental backdrops against which we project them. Recognizing the biases and limitations of our initial assumptions is key, because they often lead us astray. To find a solution, we must try different backgrounds or relational frameworks until we find one that puts all the pieces together in a coherent and often unexpected way. Consider these examples: The star that never burns is the asterisk on a telephone keypad. The man who died had no brother because the beggar was a woman. And the word that is most frequently pronounced incorrectly is "incorrectly." As these solutions suggest, context may not be everything, but it counts for a great deal.

Similar psychological principles are at work in our philanthropic understanding. What are the challenges and opportunities facing philanthropy? It is natural that our perspectives vary depending on the backdrops against which we perceive them. What works well in one context may fail in another. Systems designed to meet basic needs for food and shelter may not perform well at delivering education, and systems designed to deliver education may not perform well at meeting needs for food and shelter. No matter how badly we want to help, a failure to grasp the meaning of fundamental philanthropic concepts is likely to undermine our efforts. If, for example, we misconceive the needs and aspirations of givers and receivers, even our best philanthropic intentions will often go awry.

Consider an example, the Clinton-era federal policy that imposed lifetime limits on welfare benefits eligibility. What were we attempting to accomplish? Was our aim to promote the dignity of welfare recipients by encouraging them to become more self-sufficient? Did we seek to discourage sloth by preventing capable people from subsisting on the dole? Or did we simply intend to reduce the tax burden borne by working people, without reference to the welfare of recipients? In this case as in every other, our results reflect our rationale. Did we succeed at challenging dependent people to begin supporting themselves? Did we consign mentally and physically disabled people to homelessness and perhaps even starvation? Or did we achieve both?

Resources

One of the gravest misapprehensions afoot in contemporary philanthropy, analogous to a huge optical illusion, concerns the nature of our philanthropic resources. What is the context in which we perceive the means available to philanthropists and philanthropic organizations? In many cases, we tend to construe our philanthropic endowment strictly in terms of material property. We define the poor by proprietary insufficiency, the gap that separates their financial standing from an arbitrary minimum standard. We see people as poor, in other words, simply because they lack purchasing power. They cannot purchase sufficient food, clothing, and shelter. If only they had more money, we suppose, their lives would be transformed. Yet is money the whole story? Is it the philanthropic story's most important character?

Economic accounts of philanthropy are attractive for several reasons. First, they appear to provide valid and reliable measures of philanthropic need. If we want to understand people's life circumstances, and especially their need for philanthropic intervention, we need only measure their income or material wealth. Moreover, we need not invest a great deal of time and effort acquainting ourselves with particular individuals, families, and communities. Instead, we can simply peruse their financial standing. Finally, when a deficiency is identified, the remedy is simple—we "top them up" to the critical threshold. When the problem is defined as a financial shortfall, the solution, naturally, is an infusion of money. What does philanthropy ask of us? Above all, that we write checks.

How reliable is the link between the ease with which something can be measured and its intrinsic importance? Are the things that are easiest to quantify also the ones we most need to know? We can precisely calculate a person's net worth, but to what extent can we render human needs and opportunities commensurable with wealth? If we suppose that our only dart is money, it is no surprise that our targets turn out to be commodities.

Yet what if human life offers important philanthropic targets that money cannot penetrate? Some people manage to live relatively full lives with limited resources, while some wealthy people find themselves continually racked by want. Perhaps material sufficiency, even material prosperity, is no panacea. To be sure, few reasonable people would choose poverty over wealth. Yet an aversion to scarcity does not imply a devotion to excess. Plenty of people knowingly forgo additional wealth for the sake of other goods they rightly esteem more highly.

There is simply no guarantee that we can solve life's important problems by spending more money on them. Material goods are a necessary condition for crafting a full human life, but they are not sufficient. No matter how precisely we target our gifts, for example, we cannot pay someone to care—genuinely care—for someone else. The vehicle of wealth can take us only so far along the road to human enrichment. We should begin seeking other means of conveyance long before we reach that point.

It is important to distinguish between tangible resources and intangible resources. Tangible resources can be touched with the hand, and include groceries, houses, clothing, medicines, and recreational equipment. Intangible resources are untouchable, and include knowledge, skills, relationships, and dreams. Pondering this distinction, we soon realize that the value of our intangible resources vastly exceeds that of our tangible resources.

Philanthropic organizations' annual budgets and investments are measured in dollars. Yet philanthropic excellence requires other endowments to which a dollar value is difficult to assign. The income of foundation program officers is relatively easy to determine. Yet it is considerably more difficult, perhaps even impossible, to determine the value of what those individuals know and can do. We can measure how much a foundation pays each year to provide continuing education to its employees, but it is considerably more difficult, perhaps even impossible, to place a dollar value on the quality of their learning. People who read Charles Dickens's *Hard Times* or John Steinbeck's *The Grapes of Wrath* are not in any sense materially enriched by the experience. Yet some gain invaluable insight into the human significance of poverty.

Knowledge

Our inventory of philanthropic assets cannot be restricted to funds, equipment, and the physical plant. We must expand our field of view to include other resources, such as our self-image. Our philanthropic potential cannot be fully encompassed in terms of what we have. We also need to take into account who we are, both individually and as members of organizations and communities. And who we are is constituted to a large degree by what we know.

Socrates' most famous philosophical maxim was "know thyself," a principle that applies no less urgently to philanthropy than to philosophy. The first order of business in helping people is not to get them more property, but to get to know them. To this formulation of the philanthropic mission Socrates might add, "And help them get to know themselves." Ultimately, poverty is not the greatest peril. Ignorance is.

We make a mistake when we pin our aspirations on handling money more efficiently. Efficiency at allocating funds is no guarantee of generating and sharing knowledge effectively. Knowledge is the key. Without knowledge, how effectively and efficiently can we allocate money? We can be financial wizards, but human dolts.

Consider the remarkable transformation that knowledge can effect in even the most tangible material resources. What we have can be completely transformed by what we learn. What happened to the value of whale oil when we discovered the energy of subterranean petroleum deposits? Who could have predicted that the bark of pacific yew trees would turn out to play an important role in the treatment of breast cancer, or that grains of beach sand would one day provide the silicon backbone of artificial intelligence? "Raw materials" we trample underfoot may take on great value when catalyzed by human imagination.

We need to focus less on counting what we have and more on finding what we can create. Except for the most basic necessities of life, the things we require are not simply given to us. They are the products of human creativity. Only by combining and recombining them in our imaginations can we discover what they are capable of becoming. This principle applies to raw materials such as oil and silicon, but even more to intangible assets such as science, language, freedom, and literature. In the realm of the intangible, calculation cannot hold a candle to imagination.

When tangible resources dominate our perspective, we tend to project philanthropy against a fixed-sum view of human affairs. In a fixed-sum system, the total extent of a desirable outcome is unalterable. A familiar analogy is that of a pie. The pie has a predetermined size, and no matter how we divide it, the total quantity of filling and crust cannot increase. To enlarge one person's slice of pie requires that we reduce someone else's.

When we see philanthropy as part of a fixed-sum system, we perceive its mission in terms of redistribution. On this account, the philanthropist is a redistributor, transferring wealth or other goods from people who have to people who do not. The essential virtue of philanthropy becomes fairness, the pursuit of a more equitable distribution of resources. From a redistributive point of view, philanthropy cannot enrich the world. It cannot augment the total amount of goods available to us. It can, however, help to reduce the unevenness with which goods are distributed.

There are good reasons to question the adequacy of a strictly redistributive account of philanthropy. It manifests limitations even accounting for wealth and material goods, let alone intangible resources. A gift that enables a disadvantaged person to get an education may augment that person's slice, but at the same time enlarge the pie for everyone else. The same may be said even for investments in food, housing, and healthcare. A deficiency of such goods constrains the achievement of human potential.

Generation

Redistribution has a role to play in philanthropy's mission. But it does not play the most important role. More important than redistributing wealth is creating wealth. Instead of merely topping up our tanks, temporarily relieving the burden of want, philanthropy should strive to make us more productive. Lao-Tse said, "Give a man a fish, you feed him for a day. Teach him to fish, and you feed him for a lifetime." Such productivity could manifest itself in at least two ways. In the first and most obvious sense, philanthropy could help recipients provide for themselves and their families. Creating a job enables people to satisfy their own needs, lessening their dependence on others.

Second, by helping ourselves, we become empowered to lend a hand to others. Philanthropy should not foster dependency. It should foster giving, by encouraging recipients to become philanthropists in their own right. Investing philanthropically in others engages us more deeply in our communities. It enables us to mature as both human beings and citizens. As Aristotle indicates in his *Nicomachean Ethics*, to lead fully human lives, we need opportunities to activate generosity.

The distinction between distribution and generation is a telling one. The word "distribution" derives from the Latin root *tribuere,* which in turn derives from the root *tribus,* the source of our word "tribute." For millennia, tribute was associated with taxation, a levy paid by one nation to another, or by vassals to lords. It denoted any forced payment or contribution, including those associated with bribery and extortion. By contrast, the word "generation" is derived from the Latin root *generare,* which means to beget or produce. The title of the Bible's Book of Genesis is derived from this source, as is our word "generosity."

The distinction between distribution and generation is analogous to the distinction between payment and donation. On the one hand, we pay because we must, and on the other hand, we give because we can, from choice. A payment implies no concern for the welfare of the person to whom it is given. A gift implies concern for the recipient. If we did not care about the beneficiary, we would not offer the gift. Genuine generosity aims not merely to gratify recipients, but to help them become more fertile. Enlightened parents better serve their children's interests by providing them with a first-rate education than by hoarding every penny in hopes of someday leaving them the largest possible inheritance.

The most enlightened philanthropy aims at increasing non-fixed-sum relationships throughout a community. In other words, decreasing want is ultimately less important than increasing generativity, our capacity to contribute to our own flourishing. Philanthropy could still fill gaps, but would do so with the aim of helping us to develop into the fullest human beings we can become. It would enhance both our capacity and our inclination to make a difference in the lives of others.

On this account, the focus of philanthropy shifts from merely filling empty bellies, covering bare heads, and mending broken limbs to building richer communities. Which is a better way to distribute food: to toss bags of food from the back of a truck or to get people together to learn to cook each other's favorite dishes? Merely spreading food is a biologically important but humanly niggling goal. The proximate biological goal should be framed by a larger ultimate aspiration: to enhance the capacity for the food's use.

Those who receive food might be encouraged to cook for others, such as the disabled. The goal is to awaken the moral imagination—not merely to provide for basic human needs, but to help us become more responsive human beings. To live we need bread, but we also need to know that our lives amount to something. We need to know that others thrive through our existence.

Consider another example, that of vaccination. Communities around the world have an important interest in seeing children inoculated against a variety of infectious diseases, such as measles, diphtheria, and polio. A great philanthropic success story of the twentieth century was the global conquest of smallpox through a coordinated international public health campaign. Yet the simplicity of vaccination may seduce us into a largely irrelevant image of philanthropy. Its efficiency springs from the fact that it requires but one encounter between donor and recipient, and asks nothing further of either. We simply tell patients to roll up their sleeves, make the injection, and send them away. This is not the appropriate backdrop against which to view the most important philanthropic opportunities before us.

The word "vaccination" is derived from the Latin root *vacca,* which means "cow." The first immunization used a preparation from cowpox vesicles to immunize people against a much more virulent virus, smallpox. To vaccinate people, we hardly need to talk to them. We simply treat them as Petri dishes that generate antibodies. Yet human beings are not cows. In most public health situations, the active engagement of recipients is required. In rich countries, consider the public health challenges presented by cigarette smoking, obesity, and sexually transmitted diseases. In poor countries, consider the challenges of adequate nutrition, clean drinking water, and sanitation. In these contexts, the image of passive inoculation leaves much to be desired. We need instead an image of philanthropy that stresses active cooperation and partnership.

Leadership

There is an important difference between tyranny and leadership. Tyrants command, believing that their word is law. They have little interest in the internal state of their subjects, so long as they do what they are told. Leaders, by contrast, seek not to coerce, but to inform and persuade. Their goal is not to wrest away the power of choice, but to promote better decision making. Superficially, tyranny is more efficient because it requires less time and effort to implement a particular decision. But that efficiency is deceptive. It is grounded in a short-term perspective that does not respect the character of those being commanded. It treats people as mere instruments, means by which to achieve the tyrant's ends.

By contrast, leadership recognizes a higher form of efficiency, directed at a quite different end. Its goal is not merely to ensure that every order is carried out as quickly as possible, but to help us develop our capacity to see for ourselves the appropriate course of action. The genuine leader takes democracy seriously, not because it always elects the best candidate, but because it provides the best environment for citizens to develop into full human beings. Why are juries an essential part of our system of justice? Less because jury verdicts are just than because they draw out essential excellences of citizenship among those who serve.

From the genuine leader's point of view, the discussion that precedes a decision is often more important than the decision itself. Mere rule is not democracy's overriding consideration. In some cases, a noble philosopher-king might make better decisions. Democracy is the best form of government because it places a premium on free and rich public discourse, which in turn cultivates the humanity of the citizenry. People do not exist to serve the government. The government exists to serve the people. In some cases, pursuing that mission entails constraining the role of government in the public sphere to avoid stunting the growth of personal and civic excellence. For our communities to flourish, we need personal and civic aspirations that extend far beyond what the law can require.

It is not enough that people merely refrain from stealing one another's property. A good community is one in which we look out for each other, coming willingly to one another's aid in times of crisis. In the appropriate setting, we naturally form cooperative relationships for our mutual benefit. The law does its part by underwriting contracts and applying legal sanctions to those who violate commitments. Yet the law cannot prescribe that we contract with one another in the first place. The law can no more tell us whom to partner with than it can tell us whom to marry or how to raise our children. Where human excellence is concerned, it is vital that we enjoy the opportunity to develop and express our moral identity.

Even voluntary exchange relationships cannot develop character sufficiently. What are the virtues of the marketplace? They include fairness, honesty, reliability, and ambition. Why should people trade fairly? Because an open and fair system of exchange is ultimately more productive than one that tolerates dishonesty. We reward ambition because, within the context of a truly free market, each person's ambition tends to benefit everyone else. Missing from this account, however, are vital human excellences without which human life is not complete. These include compassion and generosity.

There is a limit to what we can accomplish through financial incentives. We simply cannot pay people to be good parents, spouses, and citizens. Such vital human responsibilities require a different kind of commitment, one that involves not only calculations of advantage, but a readiness to make genuine sacrifices. Parents who based every choice about child rearing on personal advantage would be parents in name only. Good parents care first about what is good for children. If we do not love our children for who they are, we are lost, no matter what financial incentives we concoct.

Where commercial transactions are concerned, we can always substitute someone else for the buyer or seller without jeopardizing the transaction. By contrast, substituting one child for another, one spouse for another, or one friend for another, presents a serious threat to a relationship grounded in love. In love, we matter for who we are, not the uses to which we can be put. In love, we are not interchangeable.

Love

The highest possibilities for the development of human character lie in love. Love evokes not profit, but human enrichment. It cultivates the highest of human excellences. It declares that we have a purpose in life higher than ourselves, that we can participate in relationships and communities whose boundaries far exceed our own. It says that our aspirations should extend beyond getting and spending to sharing, investing ourselves in one another's lives.

This kind of investment is not nearly as easy as writing a check. As Aristotle indicates, it requires not only that we share, but that we share the right thing, with the right person, in the right way, at the right time, and for the right reason. Philanthropy stretches us as human beings, challenging us to become better than we are. It invites us to look beyond the distinctions of giver and receiver, and to see one another as sharers, parts cooperating for the benefit of a larger whole.

On this account, exchange ceases to be an end in itself and becomes a means to another end, that of integration. It provides the infrastructure of freedom and prosperity that enables us to forge deeper and more fruitful human partnerships. We are free from tyranny, but that freedom is not a mere license to indulge our every whim. It means freedom to be with and for one another. It means the freedom to complete ourselves by sharing what we are.

An old story nicely captures this image of philanthropy. In medieval Europe, a man came upon a large construction site. He saw one workman fitting two stones together. "What do you do?" he asked. "I am a stone mason," the man replied. Then he walked over to another worker, who appeared to be engaged in the same task. "What do you do?" he asked. The man replied, "We are building a cathedral." The two men operated with very different images of their mission. One focused exclusively on the task of the moment, not looking beyond the limits of his own arm span. The other saw his immediate task in the context of a much larger calling.

How do we see our philanthropic calling? Do we think primarily in terms of fund raising? Do we measure our success in terms of revenue? If so, we have fallen into a trap—the trap of pursuing what is good for us rather than what is good for the people we serve. Wouldn't the best philanthropists and philanthropic organizations evaluate their effectiveness against a quite different backdrop? Wouldn't that backdrop reveal a much richer philanthropic potential? And what about us? What kind of philanthropy can we imagine?

2

THE GOLDEN RULE

Professions such as medicine and philanthropy cannot thrive if we cease to be professionals committed first and foremost to the welfare of those we serve, becoming instead mere trade associations devoted to our own economic advantage. One of the defining features of a profession is adherence to beneficent ethical standards, even when it might not be the most convenient or immediately advantageous course of action. Yet ethics is not a subject to which the curricula of our schools and training programs have devoted a great deal of attention. It is vital, therefore, that all professional organizations stress the vital role of ethics and provide ethics education for their membership.

Ethics is a complex subject, one to which some of the greatest minds in the Western intellectual tradition have devoted whole lifetimes. It took decades for the likes of Plato, Aristotle, Thomas Aquinas, Spinoza, Kant, and John Stuart Mill to think through the essential problems of ethics. How effectively can preprofessional students, students in professional schools, and practicing professionals, many of whom may never have taken a course in ethics, complete this prodigious task? Fortunately, it is not necessary for each of us to build our ethical perspectives from the ground up, any more than physicians must reinvent the stethoscope or lawyers the legal brief. Yet it is important that we work through our ethical perspectives at least to the point that they become a firm part of our characters. We want to know, and others want to know, where we stand, and according to what principles and dispositions we are likely to act when ethical questions arise.

Fortunately, the world's great ethical and religious traditions provide us with at least one such principle, often referred to in various

permutations as the Golden Rule. In place of a rule book or an elabo-
rate list of moral "do's" and "do nots," the Golden Rule posits a
basic principle of reciprocity, "Do not do to others what you do not
want others to do to you," or "Treat others as you would like to
be treated." Its summative moral significance is captured in a story
about Rabbi Hillel, who was told by an unbeliever that he could make
him a proselyte if he would teach him the whole Torah while he stood
on one foot. Hillel told him, "What is hateful to you, do not do to
your neighbor. That is the whole of the Torah, and the rest is but
commentary. Go and learn it."

Many world traditions contain versions of this ethical principle.
The Bible states, "You shall love your neighbor as yourself." In the
Analects of Confucius we find this formulation: "Do not do to others what you do not want them to do to you." A great Hindu text
teaches, "One should not behave toward others in a way which is dis-
agreeable to oneself." The teaching of the Buddha states, "Compar-
ing oneself to others in such terms as 'Just as I am so are they, just as
they are so am I,' he should neither kill nor cause others to kill."

Granting for the moment that the Golden Rule represents an ethical master principle, what would it mean to apply it to daily practice?
How could a professional such as a physician put the Golden Rule
to work? To begin with, it is important to determine who counts as
my neighbor, or, more broadly speaking, the people to whom the
Golden Rule applies. Does it require me to treat only other fully
qualified physicians as I would want to be treated, or does it apply
as well to departmental colleagues, residents, and medical students?
What about physicians and trainees in other specialties? What about
non-physicians, such as nurses, technologists, and clerical staff? And
what about patients and their families? Are we expected to include
the poor, the illiterate, people who cannot speak English, criminals,
and the mentally and physically disabled?

Of course the prophets and sages seem to advise just that. Abraham
Lincoln encompassed the breadth of the human spectrum to which
the Golden Rule applies when he formulated this political maxim, "As
I would not be a slave, so I would not be a master." The Golden Rule
has even been extended to non-human creatures, as in this Yoruba

proverb from Nigeria: "One going to take a pointed stick to pinch a baby bird should first try it on himself to feel how it hurts."

The Golden Rule does not authorize us to divide up the world into good people and bad people, us and them. It does not tell us to be nice to the people who are like us, but abuse those who are different from us. It does not say that we should treat good people well, but do as we please to bad ones. Nor does it divide the day into convenient times and inconvenient times. It does not say that so long as we are well-rested and feeling cheerful, we should treat people as we would like to be treated. Nor does it provide a variety of excuses for behaving badly. It does not say that sleep deprivation, or an overfilled schedule, or an unpleasant encounter with a colleague provides us carte blanche to treat people in an uncivil or frankly hurtful way.

The Golden Rule has scientific and managerial implications. It says that we should no longer think in terms of doing things *to* people. It says that physicians should avoid, for example, performing diagnostic studies or experiments *on* people. We should not try things *on* our staff, such as new systems of compensation, quality assurance, or discipline. Instead, if we are really going to learn something about others and build a community of practice in our workplace, we should do things only *with* them, and never merely *to* them. The Golden Rule does not permit us to build walls between ourselves, the people we work with, and the people we serve. We are not allowed to say, "I am management and they are labor, and therefore I need not behave toward them the way I would toward a peer or a superior." Instead, even when we gaze down at a patient or across the negotiating table at an adversary, the Golden Rule says we should see one another as members of the same community.

In fact, medicine calls us to an even higher standard. If we find ourselves doing things *to* patients, we have lost our way. Even doing things *with* patients does not capture the full range of our calling. In medicine, we are called to do things not *to* patients, and not only *with* patients, but *for* patients. The wholeness of the patient is medicine's reason for being. That wholeness encompasses not only the wholeness of the body, but also the wholeness of the person. In diagnosing and healing the body, we should never lose sight of the whole human being of which the body is a part. The patient is a transitory entity—one, in a sense, whose existence as patient we wish to abbreviate through restoration to health. The person, however, is for a lifetime, and may even influence the next generation. The same may be said of the physician. We aim not merely to discharge our obligations to patients, but to remain open to opportunities to enrich the lives of our colleagues, our students, and ourselves.

There is an important sense in which the phrase "ethics of reciprocity" does not do justice to the Golden Rule. Reciprocity seems to imply a quid pro quo, a "tit-for-tat" mentality that views ethics as a matter of exchange or transaction. This is the core of the commercial model that so dominates our thinking in medicine today, the illusion that by adhering to sound business principles and applying the best practices of customer service, we can save medicine. In fact, medicine is not a business just like any other. Illness places patients in a position of vulnerability that differs fundamentally from that of a consumer seeking to purchase real estate or a new automobile. Physicians have, at least since the Hippocratic Oath, been called upon to observe the highest standards of compassion and trustworthiness. Merely providing value for the money is not enough. The motto of the marketplace, "*caveat emptor*" (buyer beware), cannot be the motto of medicine. None of us wants a healthcare system in which our parents, siblings, offspring, and friends need to cling suspiciously to their pocketbooks.

Instead, medicine and philanthropy should consider the higher calling of the Golden Rule, a calling not merely to reciprocity but to mutuality. The psychologist Erik Erikson defined mutuality as a relationship in which the participants depend on one another for the development of their respective strengths. We should not merely refrain from doing to others what we wish they would not do to us. We should do to others not merely as we would have them do to us. Instead we should do with others what will develop in each of us the potential to become better patients, teachers, colleagues, physicians, and human beings. Viewed from this perspective, the Golden Rule encourages us to see one another not as doers or the ones to whom things are done, but as partners. Everyone in the hospital, including other physicians, nurses, clerical and housekeeping staff, and above all the patients and their families, is our partner. We are all working together to achieve the same vision.

In the effort to foster a greater sense of community and mutuality, an attitude of entitlement is a deadly poison. Physicians should not suppose that a white coat entitles us to feel superior to everyone else. Patients should not suppose that we are entitled to the physician's compassion merely because we can afford to pay for care. Such attitudes are as harmful to good medicine as the harm done to marriage by an attitude of entitlement to a spouse's affections. Mutuality does not imply that doctors need to become patients and patients need to become doctors, any more than it implies that men need to become women and women need to become men. As a woman can become more of a woman by helping a man become more of a man, and a man can become more of a man by helping a woman become more of a woman, so the partners in a physician-patient relationship can help one another more closely approximate the physicians, patients, and human beings we are all capable of being.

At times we encounter in medicine an attitude not merely of entitlement, but aggression. People increasingly treat healthcare as a cutthroat business. They argue that at least between competing healthcare providers, ideals of compassion and generosity must be dispensed with. In their place they posit more Machiavellian principles. Instead of doing to others as we would have them do to us, we should do to others before they do to us. In this mindset, medicine begins to see itself as embroiled in conflict—turf wars, battles over inappropriate utilization, reimbursement rates, and so on—and to adopt an ethic of war. We continue to pay lip service to the higher ethical ideals embodied in the Golden Rule, but we tolerate an increasingly wide divergence between our stated ideals and our daily conduct. These are extraordinary times, we tell ourselves, and extraordinary times require extraordinary measures.

But in fact, the way away from the Golden Rule's calling to reciprocity and mutuality is the path to perdition. If professions like medicine and philanthropy begin to behave as though our mission is merely to defend our own wealth and power, then we will lose the trust of those we exist to serve. Our professions will become what George Bernard Shaw referred to as mere "conspiracies against the laity," serving no end higher than our own self-interest. Against this tendency, to which many current forces are drawing us, we would do well to ponder the Golden Rule. It is only by embodying its ideal in our daily practice and calling it forth from the next generation of professionals that we can ensure the flourishing of both our art and the patients and public we serve.

3

FOUR GIFTS

Philanthropic individuals and organizations play a vital role in the
health of democratic societies, the relief of human suffering, and
the cultivation of human excellence. Yet many of us operate with a
relatively underdeveloped philosophical framework. We have robust
theories of the roles of entrepreneurs and consumers in free markets
and the roles of government officials and voters in the political process, but the role of philanthropy in the lives of givers and receivers
remains one of the least understood engines of human flourishing.
By reflecting carefully on philanthropy's philosophical foundations,
we can arrive at a more complete and robust model of philanthropic
responsibility.

Our models of philanthropy exert a profound effect on how we
perceive giving, what we understand giving to be, and whether or not
we choose to give. Some models seem to exert a particularly strong
influence over contemporary philanthropy. Four such models of giving are egoistic giving, compassionate giving, scientific giving, and
liberal giving. Each of these models offers very different responses
to the basic questions of whether to give, why we should give, what
we should give, how we should give, and to whom we should give.
Each implies a different anthropology, a different vision of who we
are, or should strive to be. Each invites us to become a different kind
of giver.

Egoistic Giving

One of the most pervasive philanthropic models is the egoistic gift.
According to the psychological egoist, everything we do is motivated by our own needs and desires. According to the ethical egoist,

we ought to act so as to promote our own self-interest. The egoistic model received its most sophisticated expression in Thomas Hobbes's *Leviathan*. Hobbes grounds giving in the needs of the self. Why do we help street beggars? According to Hobbes, one possibility is that giving provides us a means of showing off our success. The other possibility is that we give out of a fear that we, too, may someday find ourselves in desperate straits. If we do not extend aid to those in need now, who will be on hand to help us should we find ourselves in need later? More recent versions of egoism have exerted immense influence in our culture. These have included Freudian psychoanalysis, the "objectivist" philosophy of Ayn Rand, and sociobiology's "selfish gene." Why do we help other people? According to the egoists, we do not. What looks like generosity is really enlightened self-interest.

The egoistic approach to psychology and ethics is deeply ingrained in our culture. Many students in my undergraduate and graduate Ethics of Philanthropy courses find it difficult to explain why we would act in another person's interest. When asked why a mother would nurture her infant, they instinctively search for some egoistic motive. They feel obliged to point out that the child bears her genes, or that others would chastise her if she failed to do so, or that it makes her feel good. Bear in mind that these are students who have chosen to pursue philanthropic careers. If students of philanthropy are so steeped in the egoistic mentality, imagine how difficult students of business or economics might find it to account for generosity. One problem with egoism is that egoists tend to regard generosity as an illusion. Another is that egoism can lead us to treat one another as tools, undermining the possibility of a true community of purpose.

Compassionate Giving

One of the oldest models of philanthropy, compassionate giving, focuses on meeting immediate human needs. If someone comes to you in extreme hunger, you provide them food. If they need protection from the elements, you provide them shelter. If they are sick, you provide them care. If they are ignorant, you provide them advice and education. One of the great strengths of the model of compassionate giving is its accessibility. Most people have the means to help another person in need, because doing so does not require vast wealth, special expertise, or a complex organization. When we see need, we can take steps to meet it here and now.

One of the greatest weaknesses of compassionate giving is the risk that it will foster dependency. When those of us in need realize that we need but make a request for aid in order to receive it, we may become dependent on the good will of others rather than attempting to provide for ourselves. Consider the example of a beggar well-known to citizens of a university town. Each day this man used to bring his coins to a local bookshop to exchange them for paper currency. When employees of the shop began to track these exchanges, they discovered to their surprise that his income exceeded $100 per day. He had developed such a successful practice of soliciting aid that he no longer gave any thought to obtaining gainful employment.

The danger here is that compassion, by fostering dependency, ends up undermining the realization of human potential. The same talent and dedication the beggar relied on to solicit donations might have been put to better uses, perhaps including gainful employment, that would have made a greater contribution to the community. Moreover, the beggar himself might have found such a life more fulfilling.

Another weakness of compassionate giving is the risk that it will undermine the self-respect of recipients. While some needy individuals have no qualms about receiving aid, others may resent the fact that their subsistence depends on the good will of others. Some people would feel ashamed if they were unable to provide for themselves. Others feel indignant toward the public aid they depend upon. The acceptance of aid seems to some a painful admission of inadequacy. Of course, no one is truly independent or self-sufficient, and it is vital that we recognize our mutual interdependence. On the other hand, philanthropic activities that unnecessarily promote dependency are liable to damage the psyches of the very people they intend to help.

Scientific Giving

During the late nineteenth and early twentieth centuries, the model of compassionate giving was partially supplanted by another: scientific giving. This model is encapsulated in a well-known saying of Lao-Tse: "If you give a man a fish, you feed him for a day. If you teach a man to fish, you feed him for a lifetime." The model of scientific giving aims to move beyond treating the symptoms of need, such as hunger, homelessness, and disease, and focus instead on their root causes. One such root cause might be lack of education.

No longer would philanthropy aim merely to feed the hungry, shelter the naked, and heal the sick. Instead it would focus on the underlying etiologies of human deprivation. Instead of treating malaria, it would eradicate the breeding grounds of mosquitoes, thereby removing the vector of transmission. Instead of providing handouts to the poor, it would develop job training and day care programs, thereby enabling the poor to begin to provide for themselves.

The model of scientific giving addresses both weaknesses of the charity model. First, it focuses on reducing dependency by enabling the needy to start meeting their own needs. Instead of encouraging aid-seeking behavior and thus perpetuating a cycle of need and dependency, it aims to enable the needy to stand on their own feet. It also addresses the problems of resentment and anger toward philanthropy. Philanthropy would no longer be represented by images of street beggars enjoying a meal in a soup kitchen, but instead by images of formerly dependent people showing off their newfound self-sufficiency. Eventually, if the scientific model succeeded on all fronts, some proponents argued, neediness itself might be purged. Philanthropy might put itself out of business.

The model of scientific giving contrasts starkly with the older compassionate model. In the scientific age, private philanthropy came to be associated with the very rich, such as Andrew Carnegie and John D. Rockefeller, who possessed the means to bankroll huge projects, including programs to eliminate the root causes of war and eradicate infectious diseases. It also led to the rise of a class of philanthropic experts, men and women who understood the science necessary to pursue grand objectives, and whose administrative expertise seemed to make their achievement a practical possibility. The model of successful philanthropy was transformed from private generosity to vast social programs that touched whole communities, nations, and even the entire globe.

However, the model of scientific giving has weaknesses of its own. It tends to deepen the social distinction between givers and recipients, expanding the ranks of the latter. Ordinary individuals could not hope to carry out the kinds of philanthropic projects that characterized the Carnegies and Rockefellers. Likewise, they could not hope to develop the sophisticated level of expertise and organization that characterizes scientific giving. The sheer scale of the programs lay beyond their means to organize or fund. Because they could not dream so big, they came to resemble recipients more than donors.

The model of scientific giving threatens to replace the old dependency with a new dependency, with implications that are no less pernicious. Compared to huge national and international philanthropic programs, communities may begin to feel less competent to solve problems on their own. They may come to rely increasingly on infusions of capital, expertise, and organization from outside their boundaries. Dependency of individuals is replaced by dependency of communities, who look increasingly to national and international philanthropic organizations for solutions to their problems.

The model of scientific giving heightens the distinction between the haves and the have-nots, but in a new way. The most exemplary philanthropists become individuals who transfer the largest sums of wealth to philanthropic causes. The most important philanthropic organizations became the ones who boast the largest budgets. As philanthropy becomes scientific, it becomes quantitative, and the new professional class of philanthropic experts and managers develops a growing appetite for quantifiable measures of philanthropic activity.

A scientific model of giving can have a deleterious effect on an ordinary person's sense of philanthropic efficacy. When most people hear about the large sums of money being given to philanthropic organizations by wealthy individuals, they may ask themselves, "Compared to that, what difference would my contribution really make?" As a result, they may decide not to give. Likewise, when most people encounter the resources and sophistication of the best-known philanthropic organizations, they may think, "How could I possibly compete with that?" People may question whether their lack of expertise and modest resources render them philanthropically incompetent or even simply irrelevant.

Neither the compassionate nor the scientific model of giving is sufficient. Even if each achieves all of its objectives, each alone cannot reach philanthropy's full potential. Conversely, even if the greatest dreams of both are never achieved, philanthropy itself can still enrich human life in profound ways that neither seems to anticipate. To understand why, it is necessary to explore the liberal model of giving.

Liberal Giving

Liberal giving focuses not only on the needs of the recipient, but also on the flourishing of the giver. The model of compassionate giving was intended to meet the immediate needs of the recipient. The model of scientific giving criticized the compassionate model for addressing only symptoms, urging philanthropy to focus on the root causes of need. The model of liberal giving does not supplant either of these two models. It remains appropriate to respond to immediate needs as well as to help needy people become self-sufficient. However, the ultimate goal of philanthropy is not to reduce, prevent, or eliminate need. The ultimate goal of philanthropy is to promote sharing.

The model of liberal giving aims above all to transform receivers into givers. On this model, we can no longer rely on an initial needs assessment to tell us what sort of philanthropic attention a community most needs. Likewise, we cannot gauge the success of philanthropic programs by returning to the scene to conduct another needs assessment once they are completed. Merely assessing needs and the degree to which they have been met is not enough. If philanthropy is to succeed on the grandest and most important scale, it must aim not to put itself out of business, but to enhance sharing. Philanthropic activity should aim to replicate itself, to transform receivers into givers, and to promote sharing throughout the community.

If the philanthropic sector focuses all its attention on the needs of recipients, it neglects its vital role in the lives of givers. If the largest philanthropic organizations keep growing bigger and attracting more and more resources, they may diminish the opportunities for individuals and communities to develop their own philanthropic potential. Such philanthropy damages some of the very people with whom it should be most concerned. In a sense, it ends up behaving selfishly, by arrogating to itself the philanthropic prerogative. If the philanthropic sector aims to remove opportunities for giving from ordinary people and place them in the hands of a class of well-funded experts, then it works against itself. We need to give every bit as much as we need to receive.

The essential excellence of philanthropy is not the objectivity and precision of its scientific methods, the rationality and efficiency of its social organization, or even the ever-vaster amounts of money it accumulates and disburses. Programs specifically designed to harm people, such as military campaigns and tyrannies, may manifest these very same excellences. Instead, the essential excellence of philanthropy is liberality. Liberality comes from a Latin root, *liber,* meaning "free." The goal of a liberal program is not primarily to give people what they need, but to free them, to release them, to liberate them to lead fuller and richer lives. The essential excellence of philanthropy lies not in filling empty stomachs or healing broken bodies, but in liberating the human aspiration to give.

Another term for liberality is generosity. A generous human being is someone who gives freely and who takes pleasure in doing so. Generous people are the opposite of selfish people, who are inclined to take and to take more than they should. The root of "generous," the Latin *generare,* means to "beget" or to "produce." A liberal or generous person is attuned to the needs of other people and is thus able to give the appropriate thing in the appropriate way to the appropriate person at the appropriate time and for the appropriate reason. A generous person is also characterized by a certain ampleness, richness, or fertility of spirit. To act generously is to act in the way of a full or complete person, someone who possesses a superabundance that produces a natural tendency to share with others.

To appreciate the full significance of the liberal model of giving, it is necessary to think anthropologically. If we do not thoroughly understand human nature and the possibilities inherent in it, we have little hope of promoting its fullness. Human beings have many aspirations, which can be arranged in a hierarchical fashion. These extend from basic physical needs for food and shelter to higher needs for full activation of our character and intellect. A philanthropy that ignores the most basic human needs may undermine all other pursuits, because people may be left too hungry or too sick to do anything else. On the other hand, a philanthropy that attends only to bodily needs sells human beings far too short.

One of the liberal model's highest objectives is to enable human beings to develop our full human potential. Preventing hunger, disease, poverty, violence, and ignorance certainly represent worthy objectives, but they do not go far enough. For by focusing solely on the most basic human needs, philanthropy may unintentionally stunt the development of higher human powers. Merely throwing food or medicine at people is not the ideal. Philanthropy also needs to care about the development of character—the character of individuals, families, and communities. Is some ways, hunger and disease are not the worst fates in human life. The corruption of character involved in selfishness, duplicity, or cruelty wreaks far greater harm on our distinctively human part.

Consider, for example, the condition of selfishness. Greedy people are not free, but enslaved. Where material goods are concerned, they are enslaved to money and the things money can buy. They believe that the route to security, power, pleasure, and honor is through acquisition, and so they devote themselves to amassing more and more, hoarding as much as they can. If they give, they do so from a vantage point of self-interest, intending to deflect criticism, build good will, or achieve some other material advantage that can be exploited for further gain. They think that by expanding their buying power, they are freeing themselves from the constraints of want. What they in fact accomplish is to allow themselves to become ever more deeply ensnared in a web of avarice.

By contrast, generous people are liberated from the trap of selfishness. Egoists think they are the most important things in the universe, that their own satisfaction is the ultimate moral standard by which to guide their conduct. Liberal people recognize that there are greater ends in human life, to which it is a privilege to devote our lives. If philanthropy is to achieve its highest mission, it must aim to reduce egoism and enhance liberality, thereby enabling people to lead richer and more complete lives, freed from the tyranny of selfishness. To do so, however, it must structure giving in a way that promotes giving as well as receiving. The ideal of philanthropic activity should be to transform people in need into people who believe they have something important to share and who want to share it.

The liberal model of giving should be distinguished from serial reciprocity, or "paying it forward." The idea of paying it forward is that people discharge their sense of indebtedness through vicarious repayment. Children do not repay their parents for all the resources they invested in them; instead they make similar investments in their own children. Liberal giving is not about the repayment of debts. Nor is it about keeping philanthropic capital in motion. Rather, liberal philanthropy is about enabling people, individually and collectively, to achieve the excellence of liberality, and thereby align their lives with some of the highest goods we are capable of pursuing.

In the liberal model of giving, a new perspective emerges on the problem of desert. Some Victorians criticized older almsgiving models of compassionate giving for failing to distinguish between deserving and undeserving recipients of aid. They argued that people who make no effort to improve their condition, or even willfully refuse to cooperate with efforts to help them, should not enjoy the same philanthropic priority as people who make an effort to improve. Likewise, critics argued that people whose need is grounded in vice are not as deserving of aid as victims of accidental misfortune, or people who suffered as a result of efforts to do good. Such criticisms provided some of the foundation for the development of the scientific model. In the liberal approach, however, desert can be defined not only retrospectively, but prospectively, in terms of the recipient's desire to begin giving.

Each of us needs to discover the joy of sharing. In terms of the rational choice model that frequently dominates the social sciences, giving and sharing are difficult to fathom, even to the point that expecting people to get involved in such activities seems irrational. From the standpoint of human excellence, however, giving makes great sense, because it enables givers to create connections with other human beings and to pursue a good larger and higher than themselves. Real communities are nurtured not when people receive gifts from a common donor, but when people unite to pursue some objective beyond self-enrichment. Enriching the lives of others is one of the most thoroughly engaging and joyful activities open to us. It is for this reason that sages regard giving as greater than receiving.

On the liberal account, self-esteem need not be damaged by receiving. Everyone is in need at one time or another, and it is inevitable that at any one time the needs of some will be greater than those of others. Self-esteem is damaged not by receiving, but by failing to give. Consider the cousin of a friend of mine, a woman who has been paralyzed and confined to a mechanical ventilator for more than fifty years as a result of a bout of polio she suffered as a young woman. She finds herself in an extremely dependent position, much more so than most of us can imagine. Yet she is not consumed by self-pity or tortured by feelings of shame. Instead she looks for opportunities to enrich the lives of everyone she comes into contact with. Many visitors leave her room with a renewed appreciation for their blessings in life and a heightened resolve to enrich the lives of others.

From the liberal point of view, the highest aim of philanthropy is a transformational or inspirational one. The point is to inspire us to become better than we are by devoting our lives to sharing with others. Once such inspiration takes root, we begin to realize that we have greater philanthropic resources at our disposal than we supposed. We realize that wealth and philanthropic potential are not closely correlated, that a person does not need an advanced degree to be generous, and that daily life is replete with opportunities to act liberally. We realize that some of the most important philanthropic efforts cannot be measured in dollars, or even quantified in any meaningful way. Finally, we realize that small groups of people, even one person, can make a great difference in the lives of others, sometimes surpassing even the contributions of gargantuan philanthropic organizations with mammoth budgets.

Give a person a fish, and we feed him for a day. Teach a person to fish, and we feed him for a lifetime. Share with a person the joy of helping others learn to fish, and we enable him to participate in a goodness that transcends any particular lifetime. Do that for people, and we help them glimpse the philanthropic possibility in being human. This remains the highest aim of the arts: philosophy, literature, drama, painting, music, and so. In this sense, Socrates may have done more to benefit humanity through his inquiry into goodness, beauty, justice, and love than he could have ever accomplished by healing sick bodies or working to improve the working conditions of the Athenian slaves.

The model of liberal giving aims at more than satisfying the immediate needs of the needy. It aims at more than making the needy self-sufficient, thereby ending their reliance on philanthropy. Above all, it aims, in the course of meeting and preventing needs, to turn recipients into givers, people who concern ourselves more with what we can share with others than with what others can give to us. This approach moves philanthropy from social control to cultivation of character. It ceases to equate philanthropy with transfers of wealth. And it avoids the pitfall of supposing that only the wealthy, intellectuals, and managers can be truly philanthropic. In essence, the liberal model of giving cultivates and celebrates the philanthropic potential of every human being.

4

THE POTENTIAL TO SHARE

In what does our humanity consist? In his *Lives of the Philosophers,* Diogenes Laertius tells that Plato once defined man as a featherless animal that walks about on two legs. When Diogenes of Sinope heard this, he immediately went out and plucked a chicken. Returning to the classroom, he threw the bird into the room, crying, "Here is Plato's human being!" What did Plato, one of the greatest minds in the history of ideas, have in mind when he defined human beings in such terms? As he makes clear in his dialogues, he did not regard "featherless biped" as the definitive word on humanity. Quite the contrary, he offered this and other definitions as challenges to his students. If man is not a featherless biped, what are we? What is the essence of humanity, and in what does our humanity consist? This is a challenge that rings no less clearly today than it did 2,400 years ago.

One approach to defining man is biological, and this is the path that Socrates' approach initially seems to encourage. We could define human beings as animals instead of plants, mammals instead of reptiles or birds, and primates instead of animals with hooves and wings. Similarly, we might define human beings by such biological capacities as color vision, a complex vocal apparatus, apposable thumbs, and extreme development of the neocortex of our brains. Others would turn to genetics and point to our distinctive assortment of chromosomes, 46 XX or XY, and the numerous genes that distinguish us from other closely related species. Still others might point to features of our social biology, such as the remarkable helplessness of human infants and the corresponding necessity of family, as well as the division of labor made possible by the aggregation of human beings into large communities.

Unfortunately, such strictly biological accounts omit some of our most striking features. These include our intricate language and highly sophisticated culture, which sharply distinguish us from all other creatures. We are, so far as we know, by far the most creative of species. We are as much a product of ideas as of the genes passed down to us. Any full account of human beings would include not only biology but also anthropology, including our technology, science, art, literature, philosophy, and religion. Moreover, we enjoy far greater freedom than any other species in choosing what we will become. Though our choices are powerfully influenced by our cultural heritage and the choices already made by those around us, we can learn a new language, invent a new device, or opt for a new religion. To see what really makes human beings different, it is not enough to dissect a human specimen. We must see human beings in action.

This points to an intriguing paradox about humanity. On the one hand, every one of us is born human. On the outside, each of us looks essentially alike. On the inside, we each bear more or less the same biological endowment. Even if we are missing a digit, a kidney, or a chromosome, each of us is still recognizably cut from the same human cloth. On the other hand, none of us is born fully human. Whereas a newborn colt can begin horsing around within minutes of birth, human beings require months and even years before we can walk, speak, forage, and think for ourselves. When we talk about a person's humanity, we refer not only to whether or not they can walk or talk. We also refer to who they are, to where they are going and what they have to say. We admire some people's humanity more than others. Such humanity takes not only years but decades to blossom fully.

Some portion of our humanity is defined at birth, but an equally vital portion develops over time, based on what we learn. Each of us is human, but most of us are not fully human. Each of us is endowed with a certain temperament, including an innate temperament. Some of us have sunny and optimistic dispositions, while others seem naturally more irritable or gloomy. Yet our characters are largely unformed at birth, and how we are raised and educated exerts an immense influence on the kind of people we become. We hope that we have become good and admirable. Given different circumstances, many of us could have turned out far worse. We have the potential to become good human beings or bad human beings, philanthropists (lovers of humanity) as well as misanthropes (haters of humanity).

The indeterminacy of our human identity becomes clearer when we think about some of the skills we acquire during our lives. For example, each of us was born with the ability to speak French, play the piano, and calculate the length of a triangle's hypotenuse if we know the lengths of its two sides. Whether that capacity is ever actualized, however, depends on our life experience. Human beings who never encounter the French language will never speak French. Those born before the piano was invented could never learn to play it. And those whose education includes no geometry would probably never even know that triangles have hypotenuses. Just as we can learn to speak French or English, to play the piano or the guitar, or to count according to base ten or base twelve, so we can become good or not-so-good human beings.

If this account is true, then one of the greatest gifts any human being could ever share with us, or any of us could share with another, is assistance in becoming the best persons, families, and communities we are capable of being. At birth, we are capable of developing into greedy, cowardly, and incurious people, but we are also capable of becoming generous, courageous, and wise people. Suppose that having the appropriate parents, friends, or teachers could make the difference. Suppose that learning to see others in one way would make us bigoted and hostile, while another perspective would enable us to see the best in others. Which kind of friends and which way of seeing other people would we choose for ourselves and for our children?

While none of us bears complete responsibility for who we are, we each play a profound role in shaping the person we are becoming. To an important extent, the habits of thought by which we see our lives as full or empty, our selves as connected to or isolated from others, and our lives as purposeful or purposeless are shaped by our own choices. We are active in creating the patterns by which we live and love. What matters most to us? Is it the amount of money we make? The number of people who know our name or would like to trade places with us? The degree to which we can by our own fiat redirect the course of others' lives? Or is it the difference we are making in the lives of others, the extent to which their lives are fuller and richer because of our presence in the world? The answers to these questions determine not only what kind of human being we are becoming, but the degree to which we are fully human.

Perhaps the goal of generosity is not merely to give people things they lack, but to help them to develop larger, more complete conceptions of themselves as human beings, and to help them progress further along those paths. If so, then philanthropy is concerned no more with transfers of wealth than with the cultivation of human potential. Philanthropy is no more about finance than about soul craft. In fact, the philanthropist is first and foremost a cultivator of souls. Insofar as generosity is an essential human excellence without which we cannot lead full lives, philanthropy aims not merely to give us things, but to activate us as givers. Everyone has the potential to be generous, even the most unlikely of souls. Some of us may never realize this potential, but bringing it to fruition is in large measure what philanthropy is all about.

To lead a full and rich life, we need to be ready to give, to operate from a mindset of abundance. Generosity fills the sails of the human soul. Operating from a generous outlook means that our priorities are most in order, that we are most likely to be flourishing. Because generosity is so important, no lesson is more important to share with young people than the joy of sharing. We need to give of ourselves, and those who help us discover the joy of giving do us great service. The opportunity for this discovery is greatest in childhood and adolescence. Like Dickens's Ebenezer Scrooge, each of us, no matter how aged and set in our ways, can know redemption. Until death, we are always growing into ourselves.

What can we do to awaken the zest for giving? We need to recognize that generosity can do more than merely fill in gaps, like putting food in empty bellies. Even here, we can approach our work in a way that helps people develop their better selves, with a genuinely benevolent attitude toward others. The most difficult part of philanthropy is not prying open the fingers of reluctant givers, loosening their hold on their wealth. Instead it is discovering the challenges and rewards of giving well. So long as we merely do what others urge, we are not truly acting generously. Only when we grasp the meaning of giving and know its joy for ourselves are we truly liberated as givers.

What are the elements of generosity? To be generous, we must first understand those we are attempting to work with and help. If we lack this understanding, even our most well-intentioned efforts will go awry and may sometimes do more harm than good. Supplying more illicit substances to a drug addict does neither the addict nor the would-be benefactor any real good. To make a real contribution, we must first understand the void that the addict seeks to fill, then work together to discover a more salutary and deeply fulfilling purpose in life. The person best equipped to play this role may be a former addict who has struggled with the same dependency. More generally speaking, our capacities for understanding and responding to the suffering of others are often deepened when we have known the same suffering ourselves.

In addition to understanding others, we also need means with which to respond effectively. Such means are often erroneously equated with wealth. We suppose that the more money people possess, the greater their capacity to be generous. Yet this is far from the truth. Wealth is only a part, and not even the greatest part, of our human wherewithal. Some very rich people act as though they are completely incapable of generosity, and some very poor people are among the most generous souls in their communities. In addition to treasure, we bring time and talent. Simply taking the time to listen sincerely to another person's troubles can be a great act of kindness. So, too, every talent—whether playing a musical instrument, diagnosing and treating a disease, preparing a meal, providing legal advice, caring for a child, or repairing a leaky faucet—can be a gift.

Another key element of generosity is the will to respond. There are plenty of people in our communities who possess the means to be generous, but feel disinclined to help. Far from enabling generosity, wealth is often an obstacle. It is all too easy for people of substantial means to identify themselves with their wealth. They think that wealth defines them. As a result, some of them have as much difficulty parting with it as they would with one of their own digits. They regard giving with all the enthusiasm of amputation. What they need is a chance to experience firsthand how much more alive they feel, and how much life is breathed into their capital, when they put it to work for others. They need to discover that who we are and what we have is fully activated only when we share it.

This highlights an important challenge for philanthropy; namely, to recognize not only the needs and opportunities of recipients but also generosity's potential to enrich the lives of donors. Most students do not drop out of school because they find it too hard. They drop out because they are not challenged, not engaged, and not learning anything they perceive as valuable. So, too, many people fail to give not because they cannot bear to part with what they have, but because they are bored with giving. Simply writing a check is not very rewarding, no matter how many zeroes populate the amount line. Giving money is simply not the same as enriching lives. Anyone can write a check. How much of the giver is activated by handing over money? What alternative forms of sharing would engage the whole person?

What we learn from sharing depends on the mental image we bring with us. If sharing means merely handing over money, little enrichment is likely to take place. On the other hand, if we understand generosity as an excellence that draws on our full knowledge and life experience, then it offers great potential for discovery. Our unique biographies and life circumstances are not shackles that constrain us, but distinctive opportunities to contribute to the lives of others. It is above all not what we have but who we are that defines the nature of the contributions we are capable of making. Our biographies and the historical circumstances of our lives are gifts, making up a precious opportunity for which we serve as stewards. We are the guardians of creation's opportunity to express itself fully, to realize the goodness that can emerge from each particular context.

There is a pitfall: adopting a temporal horizon that is too short, seeing things in a purely short-term perspective. If generosity is about not simply transferring wealth but instead working together cooperatively toward a common vision, then it will take time to build the requisite network of trust and shared stories. How soon do we pull the plug if we do not see results? After a day, a week, a quarter, a year? Calls for short-term accountability may undermine long-term performance. If our philanthropic horizons extend no farther than the next annual report, then our results will be unnecessarily constrained. We need a relatively long-term perspective, one that looks beyond quarterly reports to annual reports, beyond our own performance appraisals to those of our successors and our successors' successors, and beyond the way we see things to the perspectives of our grandchildren and great-grandchildren.

The potential of the earth to produce life took hundreds of millions of years to realize, and the potential of that life to spawn creatures capable of generosity took additional thousands of millions of years. When we see our days against such a backdrop, it becomes more reasonable to devote our lives to purposes that we may not be able to complete independently or even during our own lifetimes. Can we seriously suppose that we are the greatest people of the wisest generation that will ever stride the face of our planet? Christopher Wren wrote that architecture is for eternity. At its best, generosity also partakes of the eternal, like a person planting trees whose shade he expects never to enjoy. The true exemplars of generosity give to people they have never met, some of whom died long ago, many of whom have not even been born, yet to whom the giver feels deeply beholden.

To invoke eternity is not to suggest that things will last forever. Even the mighty pyramids of Egypt and Wren's majestic St. Paul's Cathedral will eventually crumble and turn to dust. Far more durable, yet ultimately perishable, are the stories we tell. These include the words of such paragons of compassion and generosity as Moses, Buddha, and Jesus. They have outlasted not only the buildings in which they dwelt but the towns in which they lived and the languages they spoke. When they spoke of a place called paradise they were not referring to some future state unattainable in this life but a state of grace equally attainable at all times precisely because it is outside of time. This is what it means to participate in the eternal: to help bring into being one of creation's truest and best aspirations, the sharing and enrichment of life through generosity.

5

THE GOOD SAMARITAN

One of the most famous parables in the New Testament, present only in the Gospel of Luke, is the Good Samaritan. In it, a scholar of religion asks Jesus what he must do to gain eternal life. In the course of addressing this question, Jesus connects eternal life with conduct toward neighbors, and even more so, with our understanding of what a neighbor is and who is really a neighbor. What do neighbors have to do with eternal life? In what way do we define ourselves by how we see our neighbors, and what can we do to become more neighborly? Following is a translation of the parable of the Gospel of Luke 10:25–37 by Eugene H. Peterson.

Just then a religion scholar stood up with a question to test Jesus. "Teacher, what do I need to do to get eternal life?"

He answered, "What's written in God's Law? How do you interpret it?"

He said, "That you love the Lord your God with all your passion and prayer and muscle and intelligence—and that you love your neighbor as well as you do yourself."

"Good answer!" said Jesus. "Do it and you'll live."

Looking for a loophole, he asked, "And just how would you define 'neighbor'?"

Jesus answered by telling a story. "There was once a man traveling from Jerusalem to Jericho. On the way he was attacked by robbers. They took his clothes, beat him up, and went off leaving him half dead. Luckily, a priest was on his way down the same road, but when he saw him he angled across to the other side. Then a Levite religious man showed up; he also avoided the injured man.

"A Samaritan traveling the road came on him. When he saw the man's condition, his heart went out to him. He gave him first aid, disinfecting and bandaging his wounds. Then he lifted him onto his donkey, led him to an inn, and made him comfortable. In the morning he took out two silver coins and gave them to the innkeeper, saying, 'Take good care of him. It if costs any more, put it on my bill—I'll pay you on my way back.'

"What do you think? Which of the three became a neighbor to the man attacked by robbers?"

"The one who treated him kindly," the religion scholar responded.

Jesus said, "Go and do the same."

The religion scholar wants to know what he must do to get eternal life. He is an expert in the Mosaic law, so this is a strange question for him to pose. He should know the answer already. The text makes clear that his real motivation in posing the question is not to discover something he does not already know, but instead to test Jesus. Does he merely want to see how well Jesus, this reputed teacher, understands the law? Or is he in fact laying a trap for Jesus, hoping to catch him contradicting accepted religious teaching or even himself? At any rate, Jesus takes his question at face value, as though the questioner sincerely wants to know the answer.

Jesus responds to the question as Socrates responds to questions: with a question of his own. In Plato's *Meno,* the young aristocratic foreigner Meno asks Socrates how virtue is acquired. Meno is a reputed expert, who has presented learned disquisitions on such topics before large crowds. He, too, seems less interested in getting an answer to the question, since he assumes that he already knows the answer, than in seeing what Socrates has to say. Yet Socrates does not answer his question directly. Instead of telling Meno where virtue comes from, Socrates says that we must first do something else before we can know where something comes from. Specifically, we must first discover what it is. He suggests that they postpone addressing Meno's first question until they have clarified the nature of virtue. Then he begins questioning Meno about virtue. Why do Socrates and Jesus often answer questions with questions? Perhaps because it is only by thinking through questions for ourselves—rather than merely parroting the answer of some "expert"—that we can really understand anything.

In the biblical parable, it is important to note that the scholar is asking how he can get what he wants; namely, eternal life. He is not asking how he can help others to get what they want, or how to help carry out God's will. Nor is he asking what others or God want. His question is an essentially selfish one. He is thinking about himself. In this sense, posing the question belies the scholar's own understanding. He knows the law to the letter, but the spirit of the law escapes him. He is operating in a silo of isolation, thinking only of himself. By contrast, the fulfillment of the law would mean operating in community with others and with God. Perhaps to highlight this disjunction between letter and spirit, Jesus asks the scholar what the law says. His answer is, "Love God and your neighbor as yourself."

In its most familiar sense, the term "neighbor" means one who is nearby. Does the law mean to suggest that we are responsible for those who are near us? On the one hand, surely neighbor implies something more than mere physical proximity. Would we no longer be responsible for our neighbors if they went on a long trip? Could it mean those who are near to us in other senses, such as language, economic status, or faith? Are English speakers supposed to feel responsible for other English speakers and Spanish speakers for those who speak Spanish? Are the wealthy to feel responsible for the wealthy and the poor for the poor? Are Christians supposed to be responsible for Christians, Jews for Jews, Muslims for Muslims? This is not what Jesus intends, and probably not what the scholar had in mind either.

Yet there is also something powerful and engaging in the interpretation that we are responsible for anyone who is near us, anyone whom we pass by on the road, including the road of life. What if mere proximity is sufficient to establish a human claim, irrespective of all the other linguistic, economic, and religious features by which we might see ourselves as more or less like one another? Perhaps merely being human is sufficient to stake a claim of compassion on behalf of those who suffer, beckoning good people to render assistance. At any rate, Jesus is inviting the scholar to consider whether he is doing anything, as opposed to merely knowing the law. Is he abiding by the law? Perhaps even more to the point, is he giving the law expression in the way he leads his life?

To the scholar's answer, Jesus is remarkably direct. "Good answer!

Do it and you'll live." He does not quibble with what the scholar has said. How could he? The scholar has accurately recited the Mosaic law. Again, however, by simply affirming what the scholar has said, Jesus is prompting him to reflect on it. He is holding up the mirror to the scholar and asking, "Do you recognize yourself in this?" To his affirmation of the law, Jesus appends both a recommendation, "do it," as well as a conditional prediction, "you'll live." If the scholar does it, he will live. What does Jesus mean by "you'll live"? Is he saying that a person who follows the law will gain eternal life? Does he have in mind a future state in a different place, whose admission price is following the law? Or is he suggesting that it is only in following this law—that is, living according to this principle—that human beings can be truly alive? Are we sleepwalking through life until and unless such love becomes our animating vision?

The scholar responds with an important question: "How would you define 'neighbor'?" This formulation of the question strongly suggests that the scholar is seeking to justify himself. He is issuing a challenge, as a debater might challenge an opponent to define his terms, hoping to trip him up using his own definition. Instead of defining his terms, however, Jesus tells a story.

The Socrates of Plato's dialogues is also very much a storyteller. He inquires after definitions, but typically does not provide them himself. Much of what Socrates has to say, or at least what Plato has to say through Socrates, is conveyed not in the dispassionate, purely logical structure of arguments, like mathematical proofs, but through the dramatic context of the dialogues. We cannot fully understand what the character is saying unless we understand the drama, the setting of the action, the motivations of the characters, and even the historical and political context of the day. Socrates sometimes criticizes the poets harshly, yet he is a formidable poet and mythmaker in his own right.

What are we to make of Jesus' story? First, the context of the story is important. It is about a man, otherwise undefined, who is traveling down from Jerusalem to Jericho, a notoriously treacherous road. In those days, to travel that route was to place oneself in a vulnerable position, in part because of its unevenness and in part because it affords so many hiding places for robbers. In this story, such fears are realized as the traveler becomes a victim. He is set upon by robbers, who take his clothes, assault him, and leave him half dead.

In describing events in this way, Jesus sets before both the scholar and the reader a challenge. Who are robbers, and how do they see other people? Robbers see other people not as human beings, but as pockets to be picked. An old Indian proverb says that when a pick-pocket sees even a saint, he recognizes nothing but a wallet. The robbers could have simply taken the traveler's property, but they also beat him up, perhaps to incapacitate him or perhaps because they enjoy inflicting pain on others. Whether he lives or dies is no concern of theirs. A robber is someone who lives by this rule: What's yours is mine.

Then along comes the priest, and later the Levite religious man. What do they see in the half-dead traveler? We have every reason to expect them to act with mercy and compassion. They are, after all, the people in the community most closely associated with the law that we should love our neighbor as well as we do ourselves. Surely they, of all people, would interrupt their journey to render aid to a human being in need. Yet they do not. In fact, not only do they omit to pause to render aid, but they also cross to the other side of the road, to distance themselves from the fallen man. This eliminates the possibility that they did nothing because they did not see him. Nor did they merely ignore him. Instead they actively avoided him.

Perhaps the fallen man is frightful or disgusting to behold. It is also possible that they wish to avoid contaminating themselves in a ritualistic sense. According to the Mosaic law, contact with a dead man could render a religious person ritually unclean and therefore unfit for worship. Yet there is a problem with this interpretation. The text tells us that the priest was traveling in the same direction as the traveler; that is, down from Jerusalem to Jericho. This would suggest that the priest and Levite had already worshiped in Jerusalem, making ritual purity less of a concern.

The priest and Levite could have stopped and rendered aid without compromising their office, but they chose not to. Perhaps they were in too much of a hurry. Perhaps they had more important things to do. Whatever the reason, instead of following the spirit of the law, they preferred "not to get involved." They do not behave as badly as the robbers. They do not say, "What's yours is mine." However, they do act according to a less-than-exemplary principle: "What's mine is mine." They refuse to share any of their time, property, or even compassion with the stricken man.

Next along comes the Samaritan. It can hardly be an accident that Jesus chose to make the angel of mercy in the story a Samaritan. Samaritans were widely regarded as apostates, people who had abandoned the one true faith. In the minds of those hearing the story, there would have been something scandalous about the fact that the Samaritan outshone the priest and Levite, because a Samaritan was not bound by the law. Not only did Samaritans practice a different religion, they were also outcasts and untouchables. In the fourth chapter of John's Gospel, Jesus meets, speaks with, and even drinks from the cup of a Samaritan woman, another scriptural example of a scandalous transgression of social boundaries. How could a Samaritan, of all people, be the only one whose heart goes out to the wounded traveler and who renders aid?

What does the Good Samaritan do? He stops and cares for the man's wounds, places him on his donkey, and takes him to an inn, the closest thing to a hospital that existed in biblical times. There he gives the innkeeper money and puts no limit on how much more he will give to care for the man. With each step, he takes risks: What if the apparently injured man had been an accomplice of robbers? What if the innkeeper cheated him? Yet the Samaritan opens himself up and accepts this vulnerability. Would the injured man have done the same for him? We do not know. But it is clear that the Samaritan acts according to a different understanding of "neighborhood" and love than the ones that animate the robbers and the religious men. Instead of acting according to "What's yours is mine" or "What's mine is mine," the Samaritan exemplifies the principle, "What's mine is yours," or perhaps even better, "What's mine is ours in God."

At the conclusion of his story, Jesus asks the scholar which of the three men became a neighbor to the man attacked by robbers. He does not ask which one of them *was* a neighbor to him, but which *became* a neighbor to him. This suggests that "neighborhood" and love are not conditions in which we already exist, but relationships to which we can aspire. Revealingly, the scholar answers Jesus' question not by referring to the Samaritan, but by saying, "The one who treated him kindly." Is it possible that he cannot bring himself to utter the word "Samaritan"? Perhaps admitting that a Samaritan could exemplify a higher level of moral excellence than a priest and a Levite is more than the scholar can bear.

What did the Samaritan lose? He lost effort, money, and time, perhaps as much as a full day on his journey. Yet his losses were more than balanced by gains of which the priest and the Levite knew nothing. He gained, among other things, the full exercise of his capacity to care, by recognizing and showing to others that even those we hate and despise are our neighbors. So long as we indulge our passions for hatred, we are like the scholar, someone standing outside a good and full life, trying to get in. Jesus is not saying that compassion is above the law, but rather that compassion is the law. It is the fulfillment of the law, because the spirit of the law is compassion. The Good Samaritan sees the stricken man not in terms of his social demographics, but as a human being. He knows in his heart that they are made of the same alloy, that they are both children of God. This and this alone enables him to respond with love.

When we read the parable of the Good Samaritan, we are invited to look into the mirror of our own hearts. It is easy to disdain the characters that act badly. But suppose we try to see ourselves in the story. Who are we? Are we the scholar, the priest, or the Levite? Are we the Samaritan? Or do we see ourselves in the fallen man? Perhaps it is only when we recognize ourselves as the man in the ditch that we can actually see ourselves in the Samaritan. It is only then that the walls separating us from one another truly melt away. It is noteworthy that in the eighth chapter of the Gospel of John, Jesus, whose life embodies a mission of compassion and healing, is himself accused of being a Samaritan.

It is unlikely that the parable is intended to leave us feeling smug about our own moral probity and righteousness. Instead it seems designed to challenge us as it challenges the religious scholar. We are no better than any of these characters. We can see ourselves in all of them. To the extent that we can see ourselves in the Good Samaritan, we are invited to respond with compassion. We are also challenged to be on the lookout for opportunities to involve others. The Samaritan not only renders aid himself, he also recruits another person, the innkeeper, to care for the injured traveler. How can we not only help those in need, but engage others in rendering aid as well?

The parable also invites us to think about the importance of insight and experience. Excelling at generosity is not easy. If it were, everyone would do it. The fact that the priest and Levite do not do it shows that we require both education and practice to activate our potential. To the extent possible, we need to understand why sharing is important for the person who gives as well as for the person who receives. We need to see generosity in action, and learn to respect, admire, and emulate those around us who excel at it. And we need to gain practical, firsthand experience at acting generously, learning from our failures as well as our successes. No one would expect a neophyte to sit down at a piano and begin playing beautifully. We should expect nothing different from a neophyte in the realm of giving. Each of us is capable of learning to give well. Whether we realize that potential depends in large part on how we are reared and educated, who we associate with, and what we aspire to.

What does the Good Samaritan really accomplish? Does he merely tend to the broken body of another human being, like a kind of body mechanic? No, he also tends to the injured man's psychological and perhaps even spiritual needs. It is likely that the injured man's ideas about Samaritans will be changed as a result of the experience. More importantly, he may see the human capacity for generosity differently. Perhaps he will be more inclined to render aid himself, should he ever come upon a person in similar straits. Above all, what the Good Samaritan accomplishes is to unlock something noble but otherwise hidden in the course of human events. The potential to act caringly was always there, but only the Samaritan recognized it. Only the Samaritan brought it into being, and in such an effective and moving way. Perhaps this is the commission that Jesus, the paradigmatically generous human being, sought to convey through this story.

6

EGOISM, ALTRUISM, AND SERVICE

Some people assume that life offers two and only two alternative moral orientations: egoism and altruism. Egoism is the view that in the moral realm, self-interest rules. It is derived from the Latin root *ego*, meaning "I." Egoism should be distinguished from egotism. Egotists have an excessive regard for their own importance, while egoists merely assert that we are ruled by self-interest. Altruism, by contrast, is derived from the Latin word *alter*, which means "other." Altruists believe that we have a moral obligation to help others, even to the exclusion of our own interests. To take a concrete example, an altruist might assert that we should be prepared to risk our lives by rushing into a burning building to save someone trapped within, while an egoist might regard such an act as incomprehensible, morally indefensible, or simply wrong.

Egoism comes in different forms. Descriptive or psychological egoism asserts that we are motivated by our own self-interest, which always dominates human decision making. In *Leviathan*, Thomas Hobbes writes, "No man gives but with intention of good to himself; because gift is voluntary; and of all voluntary acts the object to every man is his own pleasure." In other words, we do what pleases us, and we do it because of the pleasure it brings. Normative or ethical egoism asserts that we ought to pursue our own self-interest. One of the most famous twentieth-century expressions of ethical egoism is found in the writings of Ayn Rand, author of *The Fountainhead* and *Atlas Shrugged*. In her essay, "The Virtue of Selfishness," she argues that "the actor must always be the beneficiary of his action and man must act for his own rational self-interest." To sacrifice our own benefit for the sake of someone else would be not only irrational but frankly wrong.

45

What are the arguments for ethical egoism? First, proponents of egoism assert that we know best what is good for ourselves. We cannot know the good for others as well as we know our own. Therefore, each of us should pursue our own self-interest, and doing so is the best way of promoting the welfare of all. Another argument for egoism holds that any time we pursue a good other than self-interest, such as the good of others, we tend to make mistakes. In pretending that we know others' good as well as our own, we diminish our own happiness. In other words, attempts at altruism only diminish human happiness, leaving all of us worse off. Finally, egoists reject the claim that any of us can properly decide what is good for another person, because doing so undermines human freedom. Once we declare that some people have a right to decide what is good for others, political liberties suffer, and we open the door to tyranny.

Altruism, by contrast, looks beyond self-interest. Moral good, the altruist asserts, lies in promoting the interests of others. From a psychological point of view, altruists refute psychological egoism by pointing to the sympathy and empathy each of us has felt for others. When we come upon someone in distress, we are moved to render aid. We sense a calling to feed the hungry, clothe the naked, and provide shelter for the homeless. Egoists such as Hobbes would retort that this apparent unselfishness is always self-regarding, even though we ourselves may not be aware of it. Even when we seem to be acting generously, we are still really looking out for number one. Either we give aid to show off our affluence, or we seek to create a sense of indebtedness in others so that they will come to our aid should we someday find ourselves in need. To which altruists counter that at least some seemingly generous acts are in fact genuinely generous. If the altruists are right, then altruism is at least a psychological possibility.

Ethically speaking, altruists hold that pursuing the good of others is not only psychologically possible, but morally imperative. Simply put, we should promote the good of others. We should do so without expectation of reward and even, when the need arises, at our own expense. Many of the world's great religions issue calls for just such selfless conduct.

These abstract ethical principles find expression in a variety of places, including the everyday practice of medicine. Medicine is a profession grounded in trust, which physicians can build by ensuring that we put our patients' interests before our own. Faced with a decision about removing a patient's gallbladder, a physician should not be influenced by considerations such as a looming mortgage payment or a patient's ability to pay. Instead, the good of the patient should always take precedence. By contrast, some libertarians have argued that an unregulated free market is the most effective and efficient guarantor of patients' best interests. So long as patients can choose freely among physicians, the market will reward only those physicians who provide what patients want. In other words, the self-interest of physicians alone provides sufficient guarantee that the interests of patients will be protected.

Physicians, too, seem to face a choice between self-interest and the interests of patients. Perceiving such a choice, few physicians have counseled their colleagues to devote more time and energy to the pursuit of their own self-interest. The medical oaths of Hippocrates and Maimonides, the doctrine of informed consent, and institutional review boards for the protection of human subjects all imply that physicians need to guard against the temptation to overlook the best interests of patients. Medical students and residents may suppose they can either do well for themselves or do good for their patients (and suffer themselves as a result). They may suppose that being a good doctor requires them to sacrifice leisure time, family life, and perhaps even the enjoyment of life itself. To do good as doctors, they suppose, they must do poorly as human beings.

Yet there is a third possibility that tends to be overlooked by both egoists and altruists. Each side of the debate sees itself as one of only two mutually exclusive alternatives, the interests of the self and the interests of others. Yet what if, instead of being separated by a wide chasm, egoism and altruism can in fact overlap? What if moral enlightenment consists in recognizing the full extent of our shared interests? In medicine as in life, it is possible for us to do both good and well, at least so long as we understand ourselves as parts of larger wholes.

Physicians, medical practices, hospitals, and medical schools can flourish if we cultivate the common ground where the interests of self and others overlap. Service is not necessarily a self-destructive activity. Nor is it a ruse to convince patients and communities that we care for them when we really care only for ourselves. An ethic of service neither benefits patients at physicians' expense nor places patients in peril for the benefit of physicians. Properly understood, an ethic of service can benefit patients, communities, and physicians simultaneously. It can enrich the lives of everyone it touches. In the final analysis, we can only do well for ourselves if we are attempting to do good for others.

What are the rewards of advancing a strong service mission? For one thing, it is beneficial to exemplify a strong sense of social responsibility. No one feels much devotion to physicians or hospitals that seem to care about nothing but themselves. Moreover, a strong service commitment helps in recruitment, especially when it comes to attracting the best people. The brightest and most dedicated people are especially keen to work in service-oriented organizations. Furthermore, shared service activities build strong relationships, and the people we meet through service projects often turn out to be important contacts when the need arises for advice or assistance. Service activities also help in identifying new talent. Workers whose organizations encourage service feel a stronger and more enduring sense of commitment. If the only thing keeping people in an organization is their level of compensation, we can expect to lose them when a higher bidder comes along.

An ethos of service also fosters improved morale. Making a difference is good for the spirit. And lifting the spirit tends to enhance work performance and increase the organization's overall effectiveness. It also enables people to identify and develop talents that might otherwise remain latent, including important interpersonal skills such as communication and motivation. Service provides opportunities to participate in key leadership activities, such as defining a mission, constructing a strategic plan, and developing standards by which to measure performance. Service also provides formative experiences in teamwork, knowledge sharing, and shared decision making.

Similar principles apply to voluntary service. Suppose members of the organization volunteer to participate in a community service project. What benefits might accrue to those who engage in the service activity? First, voluntary service provides opportunities to interact with new and often diverse groups of people, opening up important new perspectives. Because our fellow volunteers are not being paid for their efforts, they can opt out any time they choose. And they cannot be fired, because they were never hired in the first place. This requires us to build shared motivations and a sense of teamwork. We cannot simply tell others what to do. Instead we must build a common sense of purpose.

Voluntary service also provides opportunities to explore our own deepest aspirations and to share them with others. If not for the money, fame, or authority, then why are we here? What else beyond narrow self-interest makes work rewarding? By identifying these deeper sources of fulfillment in work, we gain insights into making our workplace a more fulfilling community. By enhancing our sensitivity to the needs of others, we develop habits of thought that help us better meet the needs of those whose patronage we depend on. Patients want to be cared for by an organization they can believe in, and the same can be said about the place where health professionals want to work. We need to feel that the work we do promotes goods that transcend the workplace. We want not merely to achieve the highest possible throughput or the lowest possible error rates, but to make a real difference in the lives of those we serve. By enhancing our appreciation for this need to make a difference, voluntary service helps us to become more effective at the work we do.

The goal is not to deceive ourselves with some false ideal of altruism, but to become the kind of organization we are proud to be part of and believe in. If we do the things that enhance a healthcare organization's reputation with its patients, its employees, and its community, then we have every right to enjoy the trust and respect this brings. Building up such goodwill turns out to be very important in the long run, even from the perspective of self-interest. When mistakes occur, as they inevitably do, people are much more likely to remain loyal if respect and trust are high. To achieve this level of respect and trust, we cannot merely bolt service onto the side of the organization. Quite the contrary, service needs to be built into its fabric, permeating each division and tier.

It is not enough for the organization merely to keep track of monetary donations. It is not enough to ask, "How much are we giving?" We also need to ask, "How much are we doing?" "To what extent are we engaged with our community?" and "What difference are we making?" Our goal is not to extract value from the community, but to add value to it. To optimize our ability to do so, we need to talk regularly with one another about our service activities. This enables us to learn from one another. It also helps highlight the value of service within our organizational culture, and enhances our sense of camaraderie. And it is a vital source of mutual encouragement. Service is both an expression of great organizations and one of the key inspirations of their creation.

7

DOING WELL BY DOING GOOD

George Bernard Shaw once described professions as "conspiracies against the laity." Shaw's accusation can also be interpreted as a challenge: will professional organizations rise above the temptation to act as cartels protecting their members' economic self-interest and instead put the needs of others first? Each of the professions rests on a social contract. As professionals, society grants us special privileges, social status, and monopolistic power to regulate entry into the field. In exchange, we are expected to esteem the intrinsic rewards of practice more highly than income, to regard our knowledge and skills as a public trust rather than a private commodity, and to answer for decisions on grounds that extend beyond profit and loss. Erosion of this ethic produces demoralization in two senses. First, we cease to hold ourselves accountable to a higher moral code and begin to resemble merchants. Second, professional fulfillment tends to decline.

What objectives should professional organizations pursue beyond maximizing our return on investment? To answer this question, it is important to understand the human psyche and in particular what each of us wants and needs from work. Most of us do not operate strictly as profit maximizers, focusing solely on the financial implications of our decisions. To a true professional, money is not the only motivator, or even the most important one. Pay us unfairly and we will be unhappy. But we cannot necessarily make ourselves happier or improve the quality of our work merely by earning more. What else do we want? We want to be challenged by our work. We want to learn and grow through it. We want to be recognized for its quality. And above all, we want our work to contribute meaningfully to the lives of others. We don't want to be remembered merely for the amount of money we made.

What are the professional implications of these aspirations? Our professional organizations need to extend our horizons outside the box of economics. We need to look for opportunities to invest not only our money but our lives. Even when making financial decisions, we need to do so in ways that produce human returns, not just financial returns. It is helpful when such investments contribute to our wealth, but it is more important that they enhance our moral imagination, our compassion, and our sense of community with others. For example, what can we do to help create good jobs? How can we enhance families and communities? What would make the world a better place for our children and our children's children? In seeking to be our best, we should be thinking not only of today and tomorrow, but the legacy we are leaving future generations.

How would this translate into the business model of a professional organization? Job creation should be a priority. But not just any jobs. We should aim to create jobs that provide good benefits and that inspire people to want to keep them. A high turnover rate is a sign that something is amiss. How do we create jobs with good benefits that inspire strong loyalty? In large part by offering colleagues the opportunity to grow, develop, and make real contributions to others' lives. Every job is embedded in the larger community, responding to and contributing to its challenges and opportunities. In building a business we are not assembling a machine. We are exemplifying our highest aspirations for our fellow citizens, our community, and our profession.

How can we ensure that our vision truly reflects these larger possibilities? Collaboration is crucial. Professional organizations need to think of themselves not as groups of benign dictators telling others what to do, but as active partners working with the members of our community toward shared goals. The only good decisions are well-informed decisions, and no one person or group of people sees the whole picture. By bringing together diverse groups of people to discuss opportunities, we can make sure that key constituencies are included, bring to light shared interests, clarify important information, better define the range of alternative responses, and work together to develop more effective strategies.

Good business and good ethics need not be regarded as divergent paths. Both require a common set of strategies. In both, it is dangerous to function in a merely reactive mode. It is far better to work proactively, meeting regularly to seek out new opportunities. If a stampede is approaching, we need to take notice while it is still far off, not immediately before we are about to be trampled. In both business and ethics, mediocrity breeds extinction. Excellence provides a competitive advantage, in part because it provides greater rewards. Every human activity, from playing the piano to practicing medicine, proves more fulfilling when we excel at it.

Integrity is also vital. We need to invest in others, and they need to be sufficiently invested in us that they count on us to do what we say. Professional organizations that are not true to deep and enduring principles risk defeating themselves by inconsistency and internal strife. Lacking core aspirations, they have no guiding stars by which to steer and can be easily blown off course by the winds of change. By clarifying the shared principles that are most important to us, we enhance trust and empowerment in our organizations, enabling everyone to contribute more fully.

Consider, for example, the typical challenges facing most physician groups. These include such issues as work schedules, productivity goals, on-call duties, strategic planning, and finance. How would a truly excellent group handle such concerns? Communication and shared decision making are crucial. It is important to meet regularly for open discussion of pressing problems and new opportunities. It is equally important periodically to review and revise the strategic plan. Between meetings, regular updates should be provided. It is important that all members have access to complete financial reports, so that everyone understands what is happening with the practice. Every member needs to be actively involved in monitoring practice patterns. Informal channels of communication, such as conversations at the water cooler or over meals, are no less vital. The goal is to create an informed and empowered group that can exploit its members' diverse perspectives.

Consider such contentious but defining issues as patient access and range of services. Should the group care only for paying patients or offer only those services that return a profit? If the group is truly committed to community service and the professional flourishing of its members, these cannot be the top priorities. Other questions come first: What policy would best serve the interests of patients? Would accepting more patients or expanding services be affordable? Would doing so make work more fulfilling professionally? Only after these questions have been answered should the issue of profitability arise.

Consider the formal policies and organizational culture of a pediatrics group practice I know of. It is a twelve-physician group in a medium-sized city. It employs a total of one hundred employees at three locations. By many indicators, its economic prospects appear dim. The median household income in the county is two-thirds the national average, and one in five people live below the federal poverty level. Two out of every five patients the practice serves are on Medicaid.

Despite the economic challenges facing the community, the practice provides a high level of service. It is open 365 days per year, with evening hours every day. There is an evening/night nurse call triage service. It is committed to fifteen-minute availability for obstetrics, pediatrics, and emergency medicine. It also provides phototherapy blankets, in-office pediatric subspecialty consultations, and same-day appointments for sick visits. Lumbar punctures, wound suturing, basic radiology and laboratory services, casting, nutrition and lactation consultation, and pulmonary function testing are all provided in the office.

Its interpersonal culture and sense of camaraderie are strong. New partners are carefully selected for their commitment to the written framework of organizational values. Partners practice open communication, grounded in a deep respect for the knowledge, skills, and experience of their colleagues. The practice tries to treat every employee as vital to its success, empowering them wherever possible to make their own front-line decisions. Physician-approved telephone protocols are available to staff members on more than fifty topics. The practice is pervaded by deep mutual trust, and there is an enterprise-wide commitment to excellence. Physicians lead less by exhortation than by example, and people exhibit a habit of showing appreciation for the quality of others' work.

A strong commitment to employees manifests itself in other practical ways. Though the practice faces the usual challenges of any small employer, it offers affordable health insurance and promotes employee participation in its retirement savings program. It hosts an annual conference with nationally known speakers on a variety of pediatric topics, as well as regular lunchtime continuing medical education opportunities. Everyone eats lunch together. The group fields a softball team in the community, and throws office holiday parties each year. Occasions such as birthdays and nurses day are never forgotten, and physicians go out of their way to recognize special efforts, prominently posting patient and parent comments for all to see. Team spirit and loyalty to the organization are strong.

Group members serve the community in a variety of ways. They volunteer as educators in the community's classrooms and churches, addressing issues such as injury prevention and sexuality. They serve as resources for teachers, nurses, and administrators. They also volunteer their time for athletic teams, groups of developmentally disabled children, and day care programs. They maintain close contacts with local media, who regularly call on them for expert opinions on a variety of healthcare issues. They volunteer for local health fairs and lecture through the local YMCA. They serve on the local chamber of commerce and school committees. They are active on the hospital medical staff and foundation and as preceptors for medical and nursing students. The group and its members are strong supporters of local, national, and international philanthropic programs.

Given the extensive volunteerism and philanthropy of this practice, some might think that the physicians are suffering financially. In fact, however, the members have found that their policies provide them a competitive advantage in the marketplace. The group carefully monitors its performance and documents the value it provides to patients and healthcare payers. It is widely respected throughout the state. It presents a strong case for excellence when negotiating contracts with payers. What does this mean to the financial well-being of the group's members? Their incomes rank above the eightieth percentile nationally for pediatricians. Humanly speaking, they are deeply engaged physicians who look forward to coming to work in the morning. They feel they are making a real difference in the lives of those they serve.

This medical practice exemplifies the benefits of professional excellence. Its primary objective is not to line the pockets of its members, but to provide care that its members are proud of. They have taken to heart an adage frequently attributed to Winston Churchill: We make a living by what we get, but we make a life by what we give. Professional colleagues who interact with them come away with a broader and more elevated vision of the practice of medicine. They realize it is not necessary to become mired in discontent or to lurch from crisis to crisis. They see new opportunities to put professional capital to work in enriching the lives of patients, colleagues, and the community. They realize we can accomplish more by cultivating a clear sense of professional mission, in which doing well is a natural outgrowth of a deeper quest to do good.

8

IDEALISTS AND REALISTS

Once Spanish artist Pablo Picasso was speaking with an American soldier in Paris when the GI expressed the view that modern painting is inferior because it is not sufficiently realistic. Picasso let the remark pass, but when the soldier later showed him a photo of his girlfriend, he exclaimed, "My! Is she really that small?"

Philanthropy is, at its core, an inherently idealistic enterprise. This is not to say that philanthropists cannot or should not be realistic. But the philanthropic impulse, whether to enhance the life of one person or to save the world, springs from ideals. For this reason, we need to understand what idealism means, as well as the criticisms often leveled at idealists by realists. What is an idealist? What is a realist? And what is at stake, practically speaking, in the distinction between the two?

In the realms of ethics and politics, the distinction between idealists and realists is one of the most important we can draw. Idealists believe that our thought and conduct should be shaped above all by ideals, our conception of how things would be at their best. According to idealists, models of excellence, ultimate goals, and worthy aims are the stars by which we should steer. A realist, by contrast, holds that practical considerations are paramount and that we should focus less on how things ought to be than on what we can reasonably hope to achieve in daily practice. An extreme form of realism is cynicism, the view that distrust is the only reasonable attitude toward others' integrity and professed lofty motives. Realists would accuse idealists of operating with their heads in the clouds, while idealists would say that realists are eroding excellence by allowing practice to descend to the lowest common denominator.

The tug of war in ethics and politics between idealism and realism has a long history. Aristotle (384–322 BC), though in some ways more realistic than his teacher Plato, represents one of the great idealists. Aristotle thought that the community—whether a family, a civic organization, or a city—should be founded on friendship and trust. Each such organization should be conceived as a partnership for the common good. Communities can be good only if they are populated by good people, and it is very difficult to raise and educate good people except in good communities. Aristotle believed that we share common interests, and that it is by working together to bring out the best in one another that we can each lead the fullest and best possible lives.

In short, Aristotle thought that human beings are perfectible creatures. This does not mean that any one of us could ever achieve absolute perfection. It does mean, however, that each of us has the potential to become better than we are, to realize more and more fully our natural excellences. Ethically speaking, each of us can become more courageous, more self-disciplined, and more generous. Intellectually, each of us can become more discerning, more imaginative, and wiser. Likewise, our families, workplaces, and communities can become more challenging and nurturing environments in which we perform closer to our full potential. In charting our course in life, we are better off shooting for the stars. Even if we fall short, we will become far better people than we would have been had we started with subterranean aspirations.

On the end of the idealism-realism spectrum opposite Aristotle is Niccolo Machiavelli (1469–1527). Author of *The Prince,* one of the best-known examples of ethical and political realism in world literature, Machiavelli argued that communities are founded not on trust born of shared purposes but on fear and the threat of coercion. Machiavelli did not believe that we are political animals whose happiness depends on the cultivation of genuine friendships and the common pursuit of excellence. Where Aristotle began his philosophy with the judgment, "All human beings naturally seek to know," Machiavelli judges the vast majority of people "ungrateful, disloyal, insincere, deceitful, timid of danger, and avid of profit." Human beings are not trusting and loyal, but "scoundrels," who will betray one another "whenever it serves their advantage to do so."

Aristotle thought that each one of us should aim higher, and thereby rise as close as possible to the full range and measure of excellence. Where possible, we should assume the best in others. In so doing, we help them to become the people they are meant to be. By contrast, Machiavelli counseled leaders to aim lower. To aim high is not only to consign oneself to repeated disappointment, but also to guarantee perpetual failure. Only by expecting the worst from others can we maximize our probability of success. The best system of government, whether of institutions or cities, is one founded on fear, where the threat of punishment keeps people in line with the leader's wishes. Aristotle thought that leaders should aim to bring out the best in others, while Machiavelli thought leaders' principal aim was simply to remain in power.

To understand the wide chasm separating Aristotle's and Machiavelli's views of good government, we must understand their different views of good character. Aristotle argued that things were good and bad in themselves. For example, acts that spring from a generous disposition are good, because generosity is one of the patterns of conduct that promote the flourishing of human beings, both benefactors and beneficiaries. Generous people are able to part with their money and in fact want to share it with others precisely because they recognize more important ends in life than wealth. To cling above all to wealth is to reveal a skewed sense of priorities, a disordered soul. By contrast, Machiavelli thought that there is no such thing as good or bad apart from our desires, and good is simply the word we use to describe what we want. When Aristotle looks at human beings, he sees great potential for good. When Machiavelli makes the same inspection, he sees would-be tyrants.

Machiavelli took goodness out of the equation for evaluating leaders. In his view, it does not matter whether a ruler is morally good or bad. It does not even matter whether rules and laws are good or bad. All that matters is that leaders have sufficient power, coercive force and the threat of force, to make people do what they say. "If everything is considered carefully," Machiavelli writes, "it will be found that something that looks like virtue, if followed, would be the prince's ruin; and something else, which looks like vice, if followed, will bring him security and well-being." He redefines virtue so that the virtuous leader is not the one who deserves to rule by virtue of superior moral character, but rather the one who is capable of doing whatever is necessary to sustain rule, including evil acts.

The history of the twentieth century was marked by both idealists and realists. Among the idealists we would count Mohandas Gandhi (1869–1948), who never held political office yet worked to cast off the fetters of colonialism and founded the largest democracy on the face of the earth, India, through entirely non-violent means. Another idealist was Martin Luther King, Jr. (1929–1968), who also eschewed both violence and politics yet engineered one of the greatest social transformations in the history of American life. Both Gandhi and King were repeatedly told they were too idealistic. King's famous "Letter from Birmingham Jail" was drafted in response to a letter from eight Alabama clergymen urging him to abandon his "unwise and untimely" demonstrations against racism and adopt a more moderate and realistic approach. To which King responded with a refusal to scale back his pursuit of brotherhood and justice, famously arguing that "injustice anywhere is a threat to justice everywhere."

Among the most notorious of twentieth-century realists was Soviet ruler Joseph Stalin (1878–1953). Many of Stalin's most famous sayings sound as though they had been uttered by Machiavelli, evincing a complete lack of respect for human dignity and a brutal *realpolitik* grounded in the view that politics is about nothing more than acquiring and sustaining power. For example: "The pope? How many divisions has he got?" "Everyone imposes his own system as far as his army can reach." "The death of one man is a tragedy. The death of a million is a statistic." Stalin's approach to political dissidents was equally pragmatic in the worst sense of the term: "Death solves all problems—no man, no problem." To Stalin, men like Gandhi and King would have seemed mad prophets, puny ideologues to be locked away in a gulag (or worse) and quietly erased from the pages of history.

What are we to make of the tension between idealism and realism? It is undeniable that people do not always live up to our expectations. In fact, we do not always live up to our own expectations. Are we to conclude that insulating ourselves against all disappointment—expecting nothing—is the only reasonable strategy? Is it truly more profitable to think the worst of people? In the words of Brigid Brophy, "Whenever people say, 'We mustn't be sentimental,' you can take it that they are about to do something cruel. And whenever they add, 'We must be realistic,' they mean they are about the make money out of it."

Before we give in to the cynicism to which realism naturally inclines, we should pause to recall that people sometimes rise above our expectations. In my own experience, one of the greatest gifts we can share with others is the trust that they are capable of more than they think. Reflecting back over our own lives, what did it mean when people sometimes believed in us more than we believed in ourselves? When we expect the best of others, we help them become the people they are meant to be.

One of our most enduring portraits of an idealist is found in perhaps the greatest work of fiction ever composed, *Don Quixote* by Miguel de Cervantes (1547–1616). Don Quixote is the quintessential idealist, forever attempting to apply his simple notions of chivalry and knightly virtue to a world in which others see far greater moral complexity and much baser motives. For example, when Don Quixote encounters a band of galley slaves being mistreated by their guards, he immediately accepts their protestations of innocence and frees them from their captors. Once released, they turn on their liberator, ridiculing his summons that they join him in honoring his lady Dulcinea, and pelting him with stones. What distinguishes Don Quixote among idealists is not the magnitude of his natural gifts, which are paltry, but his utter refusal to give in to despair or cynicism and his dogged determination to continue seeking out possibilities for nobility in the world.

The term "quixotic" has become synonymous with excessive idealism. The phrase "tilting at windmills" is derived from Don Quixote's habit of charging, lance in hand, at buildings he has mistaken for ferocious giants. Is he insane? He sees goatherds, whom others would dismiss for their ignorance and poverty, as fellow human beings. His trusty sidekick, Sancho Panza, the embodiment of realism, initially regards him as hopelessly bereft of sense. Where Don Quixote sees a world striving to realize poetry and goodness, Sancho sees clearly its shortcomings and compromises. Eventually, however,

Sancho learns to share his master's worldview, summoning him on his deathbed to give up the nonsense of dying when there are so many deeds of valor still to be done. Even the world-wise Sancho eventually realizes his master's genius, remarking that "good actions ennoble us, and we are the sons of our deeds." What sort of offspring are we seeking to create? Don Quixote is not only an idealist, but an apostle of idealism, and this is not such a bad calling in life.

9

WHAT ARE WE PART OF?

In our culture, dependency bears pejorative connotations, occasionally even disrepute. To be dependent can imply a state of helplessness, the inability to provide for or defend ourselves. For example, infants are wholly dependent on their parents for food, shelter, clothing, and so on. It can also refer to a state of reliance, in the sense that business executives may depend on their assistants to keep their calendars. Dependency may also connote subordination, in the sense that in the legal system, lower courts depend on supreme courts to provide definitive interpretations of the law. It can also imply a state of contingency. Our ability to pay a debt depends on whether or not we continue to earn an income. Perhaps the most disreputable sense of dependency refers to psychological or physical habituation, in the sense of addiction to a drug.

The word dependence is derived from the Latin roots *de-* and *pendere,* which together mean "to hang from." We live in a culture where independence is much more highly esteemed than dependence. Most of us would prefer not to dangle from anything. The United States of America came into being through a declaration of independence. By contrast, hanging occupies a place in the American consciousness with the worst forms of criminality. To be independent means to be free to act as you see fit, self-governing and immune from the arbitrary exercise of authority, economically self-sufficient, and able to stand on your own two feet. Becoming independent is a central goal of human development, and parents revel in their children's new abilities to walk, talk, eat, study, work, and live on their own. Often, achieving independence is a declaration of victory.

We often speak as though we see life in terms of a simple dichotomy between dependence and independence. On the one hand, we associate dependence with the very young and the very old, with the sick and infirm, and with people who lack the intellectual or moral fiber to stand on their own two feet. On the other hand, we admire people who achieve independence. We want our leaders to be able to think for themselves, and we are instinctively drawn to politicians who are beholden to no particular special interest groups. Yet there can be something threatening about a person or a group that is too independent. Complete independence is not a desirable state for a child or adolescent, and it is difficult to imagine the threat that would be posed to the identity of the United States if one of its states announced plans to secede from the union.

We recognize something less than dignified, perhaps even defective, about dependence. Yet radical forms of independence are no less problematic. Set against complete dependence and complete independence is a third alternative, interdependence. A classic example of interdependence is described by Adam Smith in *The Wealth of Nations*. He calls it the division of labor. In a free market, Smith postulated, different people specializing in the production of different goods and services can achieve a higher level of quality and efficiency than would be possible if all tried to produce everything for themselves. Yet for the free market to work, no central agency needs to tell anyone what to do. It rewards people for doing what others want and need, and it punishes those who do otherwise.

Following Smith, in what sense is each of us economically neither dependent nor independent, but interdependent? Most of us are not dependent in the sense that we are able to support ourselves and do not subsist on the labor of others. Yet we are not independent either. Left solely to our own devices, many of us lack basic skills of survival. We would be unable to produce the basic technology of communication, transportation, and housing we depend on every day. None of us acting alone could produce the foods that stock our pantries and refrigerators. Even so simple an implement as a straight pin, Smith asserts, would be all but impossible for us to produce on our own. Each of us depends on dozens, hundreds, even thousands of specialized laborers for the things we enjoy on a day-to-day basis. Each of us is deeply dependent on people we do not even know.

Economics is only a small part of the story. For we depend on one another not merely for the material means of survival, but psychologically as well. We cherish one another's company. Each of us needs someone to talk to. When we envision a complete human life, a major element is the presence of someone with whom we can live. While a certain amount of solitude is desirable, prolonged isolation is torture. Solitary confinement seems an extreme form of punishment, precisely because it is so painful to be so alone. Human infants reared in complete isolation, even though they have enough to eat and are kept warm and dry, develop a syndrome once called "hospitalism" but now called "failure to thrive." In addition to food and shelter, they need human contact. Single people grow sick more often and die sooner than married people. In short, the human organism needs companionship to thrive.

What we need to do, then, is to recognize, accept, and even celebrate the full extent of our interdependence. Each of us is a whole human being, but each of us is also a part of many larger wholes. These larger wholes include our families, our friendships, our communities, our places of employment, religious, civic, and political organizations, cities, states, nations, the whole of mankind, the biosphere, and so on. To understand what it means to be human, it is not sufficient to dissect a human specimen. It is necessary to see a human being in action. To do that, we must see human beings interacting with other people, plants, animals, machines, and organizations in a variety of contexts. To see what any one of us is, we need to see who and what we are connected to.

To know the role of the employees in an organization, we need to see how they fit into a larger organizational chart. To whom do they report, and whom do they supervise? Moreover, we need to look beyond the formal organizational chart and look at informal matrices of collaboration and authority. Some people exercise much more authority in an organization than their job title would suggest, and others wield considerably less. The same could be said for family trees. Some people never speak to their siblings, while others are best friends with distant cousins. Many of us are even powerfully influenced by relatives we never see or even never can see, such as a deceased parent. However, the basic point remains: to see who people are, we need to see the people to whom they are related.

We know who we are largely in terms of the larger wholes of which we are parts, and it is in terms of these larger wholes that we usually define our aspirations in life. These are the contexts in which we make friends, meet our future spouses, and determine what is and is not important to us. It is in these contexts that we hope to be highly esteemed and valued. It is these organizations that we seek to lead, or at least make significant contributions to. We want to be known as members of particular political parties, fans of particular sports teams or entertainers, and contributors to particular civic and religious organizations. Simply put, we want to belong, not only because it is uncomfortable to be alone, but because we cannot define ourselves and what we care about outside of such social contexts.

The adages "See the micro-opportunities of your life in terms of the macro-opportunities of your community" and "Think globally, act locally" each allude to this sense of interconnectedness. To heed such advice, we need to make an effort to understand the nature of these larger wholes. To what purposes, people, organizations, and communities in life are we loyal? Which are we fleeing from? Which should we be fleeing from, and which should be most important to us? To what extent are these larger wholes helping us to realize our full potential as human beings, and to what degree are we making important contributions to them? A single thread does not look like much and can support almost nothing. It is only when we are woven into a larger tapestry that our full beauty and strength emerge. What tapestries do we want to be part of?

Most of the time, we are largely unaware of our interdependence. For example, we may ride the elevator with essentially the same group of people every day without ever speaking to them. Yet let a power outage trap the elevator between floors, and suddenly we are much more interested in one another. We begin speaking, sharing our anxieties, seeking reassurance from one another, and offering comfort. A similar principle is at work in military training and service, where individuals endure hardships as members of a unit, failing or succeeding as a team. One of the most important attributes of an effective military commander is the ability to foster such esprit de corps, where individuals will lay their lives on the line for their comrades and the good of the unit. In both situations, recognizing shared dependence and vulnerability tends to bring us closer together.

Something similar on an international level occurred in the aftermath of Hurricane Katrina's assault on the gulf coast of the United States in August of 2005. U.S. leaders were accustomed to thinking of the nation as the most powerful on earth, frequently called upon to aid others, but never in need of help itself. However, the magnitude of the devastation led less prosperous countries, including Mexico and Sri Lanka, to offer aid to the United States. Overcoming the initial impulse to see such offers as indignities, U.S. leaders decided instead to accept. On the one hand, acceptance could be interpreted as a sign of weakness. On the other hand, it also represented a great advance in thinking about foreign aid. U.S. leaders realized that all nations are "in this together," that there is virtue in receiving as well as dispensing aid, and that the United States was being called upon to receive gracefully.

When strangers on an elevator or in distressed nations suddenly see themselves as members of a larger community, a new sense of responsibility may emerge. We recognize more completely the extent to which our seemingly separate lives are interwoven. This enhanced sense of interconnectedness and mutual responsibility can have surprising consequences, even for people who might otherwise see themselves purely as victims. In the aftermath of natural and manmade disasters, it is not uncommon for victims to become volunteers, important contributors to relief efforts in their own right. After Hurricane Katrina, many disaster victims who had lost their homes and their property began volunteering their time at shelters. They helped to rescue and comfort the stranded, to deliver supplies, and to care for the children of others. Even some of those who lost everything were moved to give.

If we gain a deeper understanding of the larger communities to which we belong, we can enhance our capacity to give, and even turn victims into caregivers. Giver and receiver can become mutual sharers as parts of larger wholes. This is one of the core principles of democracy. Democracy is not only rule by the people. It is not merely a means of reaching political decisions. It is also a way of encouraging us to make our greatest contributions to our communities. By taking on an important role in decision making, we enter a conversation that cultivates our human potential. If we expect someone else to take care of everything, we are unlikely to lift a finger. But when we are participants in the conversation to determine not only how to take care of things but also what needs to be taken care of, we are truly engaged.

If we do not recognize the larger wholes of which we are parts, our philanthropic efforts can be seriously undermined and may even prove counterproductive. Many philanthropic organizations are not really devoted to the enhancement of their communities and more closely resemble special interest groups. They may, for example, serve as advocates for a particular disease, but not for health in general. To be sure, division of labor and specialization can be as salutary in the non-profit sector as in the for-profit sector, and there is nothing wrong in focusing on a particular area of need. Yet some organizations become so focused on their own narrow mission and the small group of constituents they serve that they fail to appreciate the larger and more enduring impact of their efforts. They fail to appreciate that too narrow a focus redounds to the detriment of the whole.

Suppose, for example, that an organization devoted to the prevention and cure of a particular disease adopts as its mission statement increasing the size of its fundraising efforts by a substantial margin each and every year. Were it to succeed, it would soon reach a point where its efforts would undercut the missions of other organizations focused on other diseases. At first, such encroachments would be minor, but over time they would become more and more debilitating to the other organizations. It would be unhealthy for a community to devote the bulk of its health resources to any particular disease, whether it be AIDS, breast cancer, heart disease, epilepsy, or depression. We want to make progress on each of these fronts, but our commitment to each is not so great that we would abandon the others. Nor would we want to neglect other important healthcare missions, such as prenatal care for disadvantaged mothers, hospice care for the terminally ill, and nursing care for the aged and infirm.

Any degree of generosity is better than the alternative, but if our impulse to be generous is to attain its highest and best expression, it must be situated in a rich biological, psychological, sociological, and anthropological framework. If we do not guide our day-to-day efforts by a comprehensive understanding of the lives of the people and communities we seek to help, then even the most noble efforts may backfire. The leaders of Catholic Relief Services once stepped back to view their programs in such a larger context. When they did so, they were stunned to discover that many of their programs were fostering dependence. By simply putting food in the mouths of hungry people, they were doing nothing to address the root causes of hunger. They kept people from starving, but the price was to make those people more dependent than ever on their organization.

We define the larger wholes of which we are parts in a number of ways. One is biology. We are naturally more inclined to feel part of groups of people to whom we are closely related genetically. We take it for granted that our own offspring are the children on whom we should lavish the most attention. Likewise, our parents are the first people to whom we would lend financial assistance, should the need arise among a group of elderly people. The relationships involved here are not even necessarily biological, at least not in the genetic sense. For example, adoptive parents may be just as loving to their children as biological parents, and adopted children may show as much or more filial devotion as biological offspring. When it comes to affection and devotion, biography can be as powerful as biology.

Our sense of social identity can also be shaped by other biological parameters. People whose complexions or facial features are similar may tend to feel closer to one another than to those who differ in these respects. Throughout human history, some groups of people have enjoyed privileges while others suffered, simply because they looked more or less like people in authority. A classic example would be the slave society of the United States during the eighteenth and nineteenth centuries. In certain parts of the nation, blacks were regarded as a separate "race" and subjected to civil discrimination and inhumane treatment simply by virtue of their parentage and physical appearance. Frederick Douglass, for example, was clearly a more capable human beings than most whites, but he suffered discrimination because of a biological heritage over which he had no control.

Another means by which we determine where we belong is geography. Human history is replete with examples of conflict between groups of people who were as biologically related to their opponents as to one another. Biologically speaking, there is no difference between the French and the Germans, or between the Germans and the British, yet the past few centuries furnish terrible examples of bloody warfare over territorial boundaries. The English Channel is a natural geographic boundary that tends to create a separate sense of social identity, similar to the effect of the ocean borders of the United States. Where no such natural boundary exists, as between France and Germany, conflict is even more likely, because there are fewer obstacles to pressing territorial claims.

An even deeper source of identity may be cultural. Language, customs concerning marriage and burial, and religion are examples of more or less universal cultural phenomena that establish a sense of social identity. As Herodotus, the first great anthropologist, pointed out, we know whether a stranger is "one of us" or an "outsider" based on how they speak, whom they marry, and what gods they worship. On one side of a mountain, people may bury their dead in the ground. On another side, they may burn their dead on funeral pyres. And on still another side, they may eat their dead. The group that buries its dead may look with horror on the practices of the latter group, stunned that any human beings could engage is such a disrespectful and inhumane practice. But those who eat their dead may regard with equal horror the practice of allowing parents and ancestors to become food for vermin, rather than enabling their substance to live on in subsequent generations.

The great sixteenth-century French essayist Michel de Montaigne pondered such seemingly unbridgeable chasms in culture and concluded that "culture is king." His assessment may be taken in one of two very different ways. Some see it as a validation of a school of thought known throughout much of the twentieth century as "cultural relativism." According to cultural relativists, there is no guide to appropriate and inappropriate conduct, save for the customs in which we happen to have been reared. Alternatively, we may admit that culture is a huge factor, perhaps the most important factor, in determining our sense of identity, yet also assert that we are responsible for our culture. On this interpretation, slaveholders cannot justify slavery merely by pointing out that their parents and grandparents were slaveholders. We are creatures of the cultures into which we are born, but we also bear a responsibility to help create the best culture we can, even if doing so frequently requires innovation, and occasionally even revolution.

A particularly intriguing component of our social identity is the temporal horizon in which we think and live. How far back do we tend to look into the past, and how far forward into the future? How does that horizon affect our sense of fulfillment, the decisions we make, and our general aspirations for our lives? Generally speaking, poor people tend to have shorter temporal horizons than rich people, at least to the extent that it is difficult to plan for retirement when you are not sure where your next meal is coming from. Likewise, children and adolescents often operate from a shorter temporal horizon than adults. Telling teenagers that they should not smoke cigarettes because decades hence they may contract lung cancer is likely to be ineffective if they do not operate from a temporal horizon that reaches that far into the future.

Charles Dickens's *A Christmas Carol* offers a familiar and beautiful meditation on the moral significance of temporal horizons. Ebenezer Scrooge is a financier who has devoted his life solely to the accumulation of wealth. In a single evening, however, he is visited by three spirits, the ghosts of Christmas past, present, and future. With the ghost of Christmas past, he sees the love and compassion he sacrificed for business. With the ghost of Christmas present, he witnesses the impoverished but loving home life of his employee, Bob Cratchit, and Cratchit's crippled son, Tiny Tim, whose days are clearly numbered. Finally, with the ghost of Christmas yet to come, he sees the Cratchits without Tiny Tim, and the cold, greedy conduct of those around him after his own death. This leads to a moral transformation, and Scrooge recovers the warm-hearted, generous person he had been as a young man.

Such stories invite us, perhaps even challenge us, to examine our own temporal horizons. To what extent are we responsible only for ourselves, and only for today? The descriptions of plague time in Thucydides' *History of the Peloponnesian War,* Boccaccio's *Decameron,* and Albert Camus's *The Plague* provide glimpses of human commu-

nities where people live only for today, expecting not to be alive tomorrow. Life in such circumstances turns out to be not only short,
but to borrow from Thomas Hobbes, solitary, poor, nasty, and brut-
ish as well. People care for no one but themselves and live with the
greatest possible licentiousness. By contrast, a flourishing community
operates from a much larger temporal horizon, taking into account
both where it has come from and where it is going.

The Pentateuch of the Hebrew Bible seems to have been constructed in part to provoke a paradigm shift in temporal horizon.
In contrast to the cyclical sense of time that dominated the ancient
Near East, the Pentateuch's author(s) propose a linear view of history
in which genuinely novel events, such as God's interventions in the
lives of Noah, Abraham, and Jacob, create genuinely new possibilities for human beings that forever change the course of human history. On its terms, we are encouraged to see our lives in the context
of a much larger, even divine plan that encompasses not only days,
months, years, lifetimes, and even generations, but also the whole
history of creation. The patriarchs cannot understand who they are
unless they see themselves in that context. The true significance of
each day, each human life, emerges only when we see it against the
backdrop of eternity.

10

THE SEVEN DEADLY SINS

The seven deadly sins have been featured in a number of Western civilization's classic works, including Thomas Aquinas's *Summa Theologica,* Dante's *Divine Comedy,* Geoffrey Chaucer's *Canterbury Tales,* and Christopher Marlowe's *Tragical History of Doctor Faustus.* In more recent times, the concept of sin has been somewhat muted, giving way to more naturalistic explanations of human affliction, often drawn from biological, psychological, and sociological perspectives. Today we speak little of gluttony but much of overeating, and we regard overeating as problematic not so much because of its effect on our characters as because of the toll it takes on our waistlines. Despair has been largely been replaced by depression. To counter it, we spend less time searching for new psychological insights and more effort investing in pharmacology. In explaining unemployment, we much prefer socioeconomic disadvantage to sloth.

Yet the seven deadly sins remain useful touchstones in thinking about human flourishing and deprivation. In the *Purgatorio* of the *Divine Comedy,* Dante ranks and illuminates each of the seven sins by the method through which it is purged. Those guilty of the sin of pride, the greatest of the seven deadly sins, are made to bear a heavy weight on their back, rendering them unable to stand up straight. The greedy and frugal are made to lie face down, unable to move, in order to see clearly the limits of earthly goods. The lustful are burned in a great wall of flame, which consumes their excessive love of the flesh. The angry walk around in acrid smoke, which shows them how wrath has blinded their judgment. Gluttons go without food and drink, learning that abstinence does not entail starvation. Those guilty of envy have their eyes sewn shut so they cannot see what they formerly coveted. And those who are slothful are made to run continuously.

It would be natural to suppose that the virtue of generosity is opposed only to the second of these sins, greed. Greed, after all, is the desire to possess more than we need and can use. Who would be less likely to be generous toward others than those who feel that they can never have enough? Greedy people feel that way for two reasons. First, some of us are never able to feel truly secure, to trust that we have enough. We may have known great want in our lives and as a result developed a deep distrust of life's bounty. Like Charles Dickens's Ebenezer Scrooge, we operate with a mentality of scarcity, always saving for a rainy day. The other basis for greed is ostentation, the desire to have more than everyone else in order to feel superior to them. If we are greedy in this sense, the prosperity of others threatens us. When others prosper, no matter how much we have, it is not enough.

In fact, however, Plato and Aristotle offer a great insight when they emphasize the unity of the virtues. Greed is not the only one of the seven deadly sins to which generosity is opposed. In fact, generosity is opposed to each of the other six sins as well, though in a different way. In the case of pride, the excessive love of self, prideful people love themselves so much that they fail to appreciate the importance of others. Love of self is not in itself evil. Each of us bears traits that we are right to prize. But when we become so enamored of ourselves that we develop contempt, even hatred, for our neighbors, then we have allowed self-love to grow to the point of perversion. In pride we become so curved in on ourselves that we cannot see past our own noses. We become so preoccupied with our own reflection that we never notice opportunities to make a difference in the lives of others.

Lust, too, is opposed to generosity. The lustful person is half-blind, dominated by a way of viewing others that focuses only on bodies and the overwhelming desire to possess them. Seeing only this part of other people cuts us off from the possibility of true love. It is a kind of bestiality because it makes the human being after whom we lust a mere body. Lust is the basis of prostitution, which transforms

one of the most intimate human experiences into an impersonal exchange. To be dominated by lust is to be unable to recognize the full
human being, a person with a unique biography, someone deserving
our respect, from whom we could learn a great deal, and with whom
we might be able to collaborate on much more enduring and ultimately fulfilling projects. In lusting after someone, we are not giving them their due, not recognizing and respecting their full potential. In shortchanging them, we limit the kind of relationships we
can build, thereby shortchanging ourselves as well.

Anger involves a distinct lack of generosity. To feel wrathful toward someone else is to want to hurt them beyond what is fair and
just. There is a difference between insisting that guilty people receive
their just deserts and wanting to see them suffer because they seem
to have wronged us in some way. When we give our anger full rein,
we allow our moral perspective to become grievously distorted, so
distorted that we prefer the perverse pleasure of seeing other people
suffer to the health of a good relationship with them. Anger tends
to isolate us, cutting us off from others. It may lead us to deny the
many good features of the objects of our wrath, and even to ignore
their generous overtures of reconciliation. The perceived slight is
blown so out of proportion that we are prepared to sacrifice our relationship and the possibility of any future relationship merely to satisfy our appetite for vengeance. Such an attitude bespeaks not generosity but an extreme form of selfishness.

Gluttony is incompatible with generosity. Overindulging in food,
drink, or other intoxicants means that we have mistaken the lower for
the higher. Instead of relishing the fine conversation that characterizes a truly memorable meal, we have lowered our sights to the food
and drink alone. We have become, in Aristotle's words, not connoisseurs of conviviality, but mere grazing cattle, eaters who happen to
savor our food in one another's presence. The person who drinks to
excess has ceased to value the openness and spontaneity that a good
glass of spirits may foster and instead become fixated on the mere
act of drinking itself, or the state of oblivion to which it eventually
gives rise. An insensible person is no use to anyone. We must eat to
live, that much is certain. Yet it is a grave mistake to begin eating as

though we live to eat. To paraphrase scripture, it is not so much by what goes into our mouths that we define ourselves as human beings, but by what comes out of them.

Envy is closely related to greed, and equally at odds with generosity. Envious and jealous people see what others have and want it for themselves. They are constantly appraising their own state of well-being by the standards of others. If our neighbor gets a new car, then we must have one too. If our neighbor's children win a prize, then ours must win an even bigger one. So caught up are we in keeping up with the Joneses that many of us would prefer to receive $100 per week so long as everyone else receives only $90 than to receive $150 per week when everyone else receives $160. Deeply envious people have largely ceased to care about their own good and have instead become caught up with depriving other people of theirs. Underlying this invidiousness is frank hostility, which leads us to rejoice in the deprivation of others. This is the very opposite of generosity, in which we rejoice in others' abundance and flourishing.

The last of the seven deadly sins is sloth, which is no less opposed to generosity than the others. What happens when we give in to sloth? First, it places an unfair burden on others to work harder. This not only undermines the performance of our organizations but also foments resentment. Second, it means depriving others of our potential contributions. We are capable of much more than we achieve in slumber or idle amusement. To be sure, rest and recreation are necessary, but not in excess, and especially not if they cut us off from others we are capable of helping. Moreover, idle amusements do not cultivate our capabilities. They render us less fit, less industrious, less ambitious. Instead of developing each of us as a human being, they make us less as people. We are fortunate that we cannot become fit by taking a pill and that we cannot become wise by sleeping on a book. Why? Because it is only through active effort that we develop that part of our character that makes us useful to ourselves and others. A full life is devoted to the energetic pursuit of the things most worth sharing.

Each of the seven deadly sins represents a destructive habit, a way of seeing, acting, and being that tends to foreclose the possibilities for human flourishing latent in our daily lives. When we give in to them, we make mountains out of molehills, take and hoard when we should give and share, and cut ourselves off from the very people in whose goodness we should rejoice. Each of the seven deadly sins implies a kind of myopia, an inability to see the larger contexts in which we live and act, and an inwardly directed gaze that distracts us from the larger purposes to which we could be devoting our lives. They are called deadly not primarily because they consign us to the fiery pits of hell. As Dante indicates by the purgatives he portrays, no such sinner is irredeemable. Instead, the sins are called deadly because in indulging in them we deaden ourselves to the highest and best ends in life. They are called deadly because the more time and energy we devote to them, the less living we do each and every day.

11

MATERIALIST PHILANTHROPY

How do we assay giving? Is its magnitude directly correlated with the amount of money that changes hands between giver and receiver? Is our capacity to give directly correlated with the amount of wealth we possess? When we talk about the most generous people of our own day, are we talking about the people who have written the largest checks? When we seek out the people with the potential to do the most good, are we looking for the ones with the thickest wallets and largest investment portfolios? By this sort of measure, Andrew Carnegie would have been the greatest giver of his generation, John D. Rockefeller of his, and people like Bill Gates and Warren Buffett would be the most generous people of our own day. To determine where the greatest philanthropic potential lies, we would merely need to consult a listing of the nation's wealthiest people.

There is little question that this economic model dominates most discussions of philanthropy in the news media. Whether it be the final score of a sporting contest, the size of a fisherman's catch, or the salary of a corporate executive, we love to quantify and compare the magnitude of various human achievements. And we are especially interested in who comes out on top. From the world's sexiest man or woman to the most prestigious college or university to America's best- and worst-dressed people, we are fascinated by superlatives. In our zest for such rankings, we happily overlook the inconvenient fact that the rankings tend to change substantially from year to year even though the ranks of the competitors undergo very little turnover. Where philanthropy is concerned, such rankings may even prove salutary, if the spirit of competition spurs us to greater generosity.

Yet if such accounts were true, it would imply not only that those with the most property have the most to give, but that those with the least property are most in need. The rich are rich because they have the most stuff, and the poor are poor because they don't have enough stuff. On the one hand, this is obviously true. We assess wealth and poverty by economic means, and we always have. But there are consequences to assaying our giving by how much stuff we transfer to others and assaying our potential to give by how much stuff we possess. Some of these consequences are problematic. A richer and more complete account of giving would take into account not only the economic dimensions of sharing and generosity, but others too. A really robust and vibrant philanthropy would see itself as concerned with something more than merely moving stuff from one person or group of people to another.

If material goods were the sole route to human flourishing, it would make sense to posit them as the sole currency of philanthropy. The same could be said if material goods were the most important route. But suppose material goods are neither the sole nor the most important route to human flourishing. Suppose giving people more stuff may not make them better off in the long run or in any deep sense. Suppose in fact that giving us more stuff not only does not enrich us, but often leaves us worse off, at least if it is done incorrectly. We can admit that a certain level of material prosperity is very important, perhaps even essential, to human flourishing. People who do not have enough food to eat are unlikely to fare well. Yet we cannot necessarily render ourselves or anyone else better off by merely piling more food on them.

We cannot assay the quality of someone's life by the amount of money they earn or the amount of wealth they possess. There are people of modest means who are leading very rich lives, and there are people of great wealth who are leading impoverished ones. There are cases of lottery winners, entertainers, and sports stars whose lives were not only not enriched by sudden wealth, but actually undone by it. Each of us might shudder to think what would have become of us had we suddenly become rich at the age of eighteen or twenty-one years. Would we be better people? Would the magnitude of our contribution in life have been augmented by the wealth? Or would many of us have found ourselves sinking deeper and deeper into self-absorbed amusement? We can only hope that we would do better today, having achieved a higher level of maturity.

To assay the kinds of lives we are leading, standard of living is a useful parameter. But it is not the whole story. In fact, it is not even the largest part of the story. In many ways, poverty seems to incite vice, at least when it comes to such crimes as theft. Wealthy people are much less likely than poor people to commit various types of property crimes. No one is suggesting that the only route to a virtuous life is to take a vow of poverty. It is difficult to develop fully as human beings when we can think about little more than where our next meal is coming from. While the amount of wealth the wisest people would choose to possess is very much open to question, it seems likely that at least a moderate degree of material comfort would be desirable to everyone.

Materialism is a term of multiple meanings. In philosophy, it can refer to the idea that physical matter is the only real substance, and that everything else, including our thoughts and feelings, must be explained in terms of physical phenomena. A materialist would see human happiness and misery as manifestations of neurochemical states, and might even see manipulating neurochemistry as the most promising way of addressing them. In another sense, materialism refers to the idea that physical well-being and worldly possessions are the greatest goods we can attain in life. Benjamin Franklin famously wrote, "Early to bed and early to rise, makes a man healthy, wealthy, and wise." A thoroughgoing materialist would have little interest in the third of these benefits. If we are healthy and wealthy, what else do we need? The third sense of materialism is a pejorative one; namely, an excessive preoccupation with worldly concerns.

Materialistic philanthropy does not focus all its attention on neurobiology, but it does see physical well-being and worldly possessions as the foundation of all philanthropic activity. On this account, we could easily assay our flourishing by measuring our standard of living. To the extent that education entered the picture, it would do so as a means of elevating our material conditions. Education would be desirable not as a good in itself, but because the educated tend to enjoy higher standards of living than the uneducated. The arts might be more problematic, unless we could demonstrate that they produce economic benefits. At least in the sense that they afford opportunities for ostentation, to show off how well off we are, they might be useful in confirming our sense of well-being.

To assess philanthropic performance, we could merely measure the amount of money that changes hands through giving. We could total up all the money people gave at church, to the United Way, to beggars on the street, and so on. We could then compare our performance to that of other similar groups, and to our own past levels of giving. Are we more or less generous than the family across the street, the church down the road, or the nation across the border? Are we giving more or less than we did last year? The allure of this approach is that it seems to provide concrete and easily comparable results. To show that we are better than others or making progress over time, all we need to do is write out a larger check. What is philanthropy? On this account, it is the voluntary transfer of money without regard to personal gain.

Of course, money and property cannot be the whole story of a materialistic philanthropy. Our economy produces not only goods but services, and we would need to take those services into account to get a complete picture of the value of our giving. This can be difficult, but a philanthropy of money would have no alternative. We might, for example, attempt to determine the economic value of such activities as babysitting a child for a day, making baked goods for the church social, or visiting a neighbor in the hospital, based on the comparable value of such activities were they purchased in the labor market. Though defining such gifts of service is more technically difficult than simply seeing how many dollars change hands, the goal remains the same: to assay philanthropy according to materialistic methods, ultimately quantifiable in dollars and cents.

If, however, materialistic accounts neglect certain aspects of a richly human life, then we should be cautious about adopting them as our standard. Other approaches to philanthropy may be more demanding to understand and control, but this alone does not justify their abandonment in favor of a purely materialistic account. More dangerous than a philanthropic discourse that leaves us unsure whether we are doing better than our competitors or making any progress from year to year is an account that demeans or even corrupts philanthropic discourse and those who would give. If material goods are inherently limited as a means to human enrichment, then we have no choice but to look beyond material assessments of our philanthropic activity. In medicine, pulse rate, blood pressure, and temperature are easy to measure, but they do not tell the whole story of human health. Likewise, in philanthropy, dollars do not tell the whole story of human giving.

We can distinguish between two different types of relationships: exchange relationships and gift relationships. In exchange relationships, we give with the expectation of receiving something in return. More precisely, we expect to receive something more or less commensurate in value with what we are giving. Exchange relationships characterize a large part of our economic lives. When we purchase a commodity, whether a big-ticket item such as a house or an automobile, or something more modest such as a beverage or a newspaper, we expect to pay a fair price. We do not want to be taken advantage of, to receive too little value for what we paid. The same goes for the purchase of services. Whether paying for a household repair or a college education, we want to receive good value for our money. We want the exchange to be fair.

By contrast, gifts are given with no expectation of return. When we volunteer our time to coach a youth sports team, assist at a disaster shelter, or teach a Sunday school class, we do so without expecting to be paid or to receive any other good or service in return. The same is true when we give away money or goods to needy strangers, friends, relatives, and charitable organizations. Giving a gift means that we are no longer engaged in the calculation of return. To be sure, we still want to make sure that our gift produces an adequate benefit. For example, we would not choose to give our time, talent, or treasure to people who would gain little or nothing from our efforts. To take an extreme case, none of us would choose to donate our time to teach household pets how to operate a computer. But the return on investment we expect is for the recipient, not the giver.

Some would argue that there is no such thing as a true gift or that acts of true giving are very rare. Psychologists, sociologists, and economists going at least all the way back to Thomas Hobbes have argued that every gift, or at least nearly every gift, is in fact intended to produce a return on investment for the giver. One such return is pride. By giving we show how powerful, wealthy, or generous we are. Another is insurance. By giving to another person, especially a close relative or friend, we help to ensure that they will be inclined to help us should we ever find ourselves in need. Another still is genetic. By helping those who share our genes, especially our children and our nieces and nephews, we help to ensure that genes like ours carry on in the next generation.

Perhaps the most insidious argument for self-interested giving concerns the satisfaction that givers derive from the act of giving. When we ask givers how they feel about their generosity, many say that it is one of the most enjoyable and fulfilling things they do. To those who regard giving with a jaundiced eye, this implies that we reap a substantial psychological reward from helping others. This in turn implies that we are not really giving. Because giving makes us feel good, what seems to be a gift is in fact another kind of exchange relationship. We help the recipient, and the recipient's gratitude, admiration, or flourishing under our care provides the return. If we did not feel good about giving, the cynic would argue, we would not do it. Therefore, all giving, except rare gifts that really hurt the giver, is essentially self-interested.

One serious flaw in this point of view is that generosity, like all human excellences, is not only not undone by pleasure, but is in fact characterized by pleasure. When we think of a generous person, someone for whom it is almost second nature to give and to give well, we think of someone who gives joyfully. Truly generous people do not have to grit their teeth or pinch themselves to part with what they have. People who did would not be truly generous. At best, they would be attempting to act as if they were generous. Truly generous people derive great pleasure from giving well, because they truly want to give. Yet they are not selfish. The pleasure is not what they have in mind when they choose to give. They give to help others, and the pleasure is a kind of by-product.

A selfish giver, if there were such a thing, would be the one who put the pleasure to be derived from the gift ahead of the needs of the recipient. Suppose, for example, that parents paid for their child's college education not because they put the interests of the child first, but because of the pride and satisfaction they expect to derive from seeing their child graduate. In this case and others like it, people might be giving for the pleasure. In fact, however, this pleasure is not the pleasure of giving. A truly generous person finds fulfillment in the act of giving itself. To put the pleasure itself first is to forfeit the genuine joy that can come from giving. If we choose to give because we expect to get a kick out of it, and the choice of the recipient is merely arbitrary, then we are not really giving generously in the first place, and the joy of giving will be lost to us.

Exchange relationships do not develop human character very far. We may strike bargains with others—"I will pay this amount of money for that car." Or we may strike bargains with ourselves—"I will donate this amount of money not to feel stingy anymore." In either case, we are engaged in a kind of exchange relationship, striking bargains of one type or another. This is not to say that exchange relationships are necessarily bad for us. Faring well in such relationships generally requires the practice of certain exchange-related virtues, such as fairness, honesty, reliability, and ambition. Most of us do not want to trade with others who have a reputation as cheats or liars. Yet each of these virtues is essentially self-referential and self-interested. We cultivate them because it is best for us to do so.

Yet there are important limits on how much we can achieve, humanly speaking, through exchange relationships. For example, we cannot really pay people to be good parents, spouses, or children. We cannot pay them to be good citizens, good neighbors, and good friends. And we cannot pay ourselves to be good human beings. From the standpoint of genuine friendship, it would be a disaster to offer to pay someone to be our friend. How much would it cost? As soon as such calculations enter into the relationship, it has ceased to be a true friendship and has become a mere bargain. Prostitution is an example of such cheapening and denigration of the gift relationship, where an intimate and precious bond is irretrievably cheapened and corrupted by having a price put on it.

In a sense, to flourish as human beings requires that we have the opportunity to sacrifice ourselves. Sacrifice in this sense does not entail injury or destruction. It does mean that we must give freely of ourselves without expectation of return. The word "sacrifice" is derived from Latin roots meaning "to make sacred." That which is sacred is consecrated, made holy. To sacrifice is not to throw away or waste something, but to commit it to a higher purpose. And this is what we do when we give in the best sense. We take what we have in the way of time, talent, or treasure and commit it to a purpose larger than ourselves. We make more of what we are giving than if we merely kept it for ourselves.

To sacrifice in this sense, we must know and understand that for which we are giving. To know what our gift is for, we must know the particular person, group of people, or larger purpose for which we give. In this respect, gift relationships are very different from exchange relationships. In an exchange relationship, we can always substitute someone else. What we can buy from one seller we can, in principle, buy from any seller. Vendors sell their goods or services to anyone who can pay the price. In a gift relationship, by contrast, we are giving to this particular recipient and not to any other. We are giving because we understand the benefits that will flow to this particular person in this particular set of circumstances. To substitute someone else would require a different gift.

We might think that the bargaining that characterizes exchange relationships makes them considerably more challenging than giving. Think of the arduous negotiations that often characterize the purchase of a house or car. In fact, however, giving can be equally intense, or even more intense. To give well, as Aristotle suggested, means giving the appropriate thing in the appropriate amount to the appropriate person at the appropriate time in the appropriate way for the appropriate reason. In other words, to give well means that we must really know what we are doing. This implies that we thoroughly understand both our prospective recipient and the circumstances of his or her life. In one case, giving five dollars might be appropriate. In another, five thousand dollars might be the appropriate amount. In still another, giving our time or talent might be better than any amount of money.

We should distinguish between two different types of philanthropic resources. On the one hand, there are material resources. These include money, equipment, facilities, and even personnel and time, at least insofar as we can contract for someone's services. On the other hand, there are psychological resources, which include knowledge, compassion, commitment, and even enthusiasm. It is difficult for us to be effective givers if we lack the material resources necessary to do so. We cannot feed hungry people unless we have food. We cannot prevent certain communicable diseases unless we have the appropriate immunizations and the equipment and personnel necessary to administer them. We cannot address the problem of ignorance without schools, including a physical plant, books, and teachers. Material resources are often crucial.

Yet material resources alone are not enough. We can provide a surplus of material resources, yet discover that our philanthropic efforts fail miserably. In the hands of a corrupt or incompetent government, food aid can rot on the docks. If the people delivering medical equipment and supplies do not know what they are doing, the aid can be wasted. And schools can become mere instruments of indoctrination and tyranny if the people running them are more committed to power than knowledge. Even if not a single ounce of food spoils, every drop of medicine is delivered to patients, and every seat in the classroom is occupied, resources can be wasted. For material resources to be used to their fullest potential, both as effectively and efficiently as possible, a more than purely material understanding is called for.

Psychological resources are crucial. Even the most materially well off among us will remain philanthropically inert if we feel no sense of calling to give. Charles Dickens's *A Christmas Carol* and Leo Tolstoy's "Master and Man" provide inspiring stories of a personal transformation from selfishness and acquisitiveness to generosity and warmth of spirit. Scrooge and Vasily discover that in the final analysis, the riches they have been heaping up for themselves really amount to very little. Instead of measuring themselves strictly by their bank accounts and investment portfolios, they find a new way of assessing their lives, according to the love in their hearts and their contributions to the lives of others. If Dickens and Tolstoy are right, each of us is moved by a desire to lead a life of significance, to be known and to know ourselves as a force for good in the world.

Psychological resources can transform material resources in another respect. Even in the realm of exchange relations, we can trade goods and services in ways that are not only fair and mutually convenient, but also conducive to human flourishing. Instead of being ends in themselves, commercial transactions can serve as a means through which to foster human relationships. How do we interact with the people we pay and who pay us? Do we treat them with respect? Do we recognize their dignity? Are we aware that they too are someone's son or daughter, wife or husband, father or mother? Some particularly generous people see in such interactions an opportunity to promote a general spirit of good will, and perhaps even to find a new friend. In exchanging with one another, we can also grow closer to one another.

Intangible assets are often worth more than tangible ones. If we base our choice of career on a strictly economic analysis, then we are missing the boat. While few of us can afford to ignore the issue of compensation, wages should not be the most important factor in determining which position to accept. At our best, we want more from our jobs than a mere paycheck. A corner office and large bonus are not sufficient to build deep commitment and long-term fulfillment. We need to grow and develop through our work, to realize a sense of genuine achievement, to be recognized for what we do, to engage our best knowledge and talents, and to contribute to the well-being of others. We need to know that work is making a difference in our lives and providing us the opportunity to make a difference in the lives of others.

What we have is less important than who we are and what we do. Consider the difference between three people with musical interests. One person collects a particular type of musical instrument. Nothing makes this collector happier than adding a new piece to his collection, particularly if it is rare, and he spends much of his time researching the market and plotting his next acquisition. Another person, by contrast, aspires to play this type of instrument as well as he possibly can. He is less interested in seeing the instrument on display than in hearing the music it can produce, and especially in playing it himself. The third person loves not only to play the instrument, but to compose music for it. Who makes the most of what he has?

If intangible resources are more important than tangible ones, then generosity of spirit is more important than generosity of pocket-book. If we not only tolerate but celebrate inequality, it is not be-cause it authorizes great wealth, but because it is a necessary condi-tion for certain types of generosity. If we were all equal, there would be nothing to give. We celebrate wealth not because it is the natural outcome of greed, but because it gives us means to make a differ-ence for others. In the final analysis, we cannot get rid of poverty by giving people money, any more than we can make people generous by persuading them to give their money away. It is by the heart, not the pocketbook, that generosity is ultimately assayed. Imagination is more powerful than any material assets, and human insight is more important than wealth.

In the contemporary world of philanthropy, it is not uncommon to hear people decrying the amateurism that pervades the so-called third sector. Such critics argue that philanthropy needs to operate in a much more businesslike fashion, with more transparency and ac-countability and greater clarity in the specification and assessment of outcomes. In short, they call for the professionalization of the field. In their defense, there is little doubt that many philanthropic orga-nizations would benefit from improved management. The injection of a larger dose of sound business practices would undoubtedly prove helpful in many respects. Yet the spirit of amateurism is a resource that philanthropy cannot do without. Amateurs act generously not because they are paid, but because they love to do so. True philan-thropy, the love of humankind, must be the work of such people.

12

WHOEVER HAS WILL RECEIVE MORE

Generosity is good for us as well as for those we are trying to help. First, generosity helps us to realize that we can live quite happily without being rich. Some of the richest people I have known seemed to spend most of their time thinking about how to accumulate more wealth. To borrow from William Wordsworth, "Getting and spending, we lay waste our powers." Second, being generous helps us to recognize and appreciate what we really have. Money can come and go, which is why we have to lock it up in a safe, but higher goods such as knowledge become a permanent part of who we are. Third, giving helps us to understand that the most important things in life do not diminish, but instead actually grow, in the sharing. For example, if you give me five dollars, you are five dollars poorer, but if you help me learn something important, such as how to be a more generous person, we are both better off. He who teaches learns twice.

Consider the field of medicine. Should college students who embark on a career in medicine feel jealous of college chums who, instead of devoting seven or eight years of their lives to learning how to care for the sick, went into business and are now millionaires? To be sure, the business tycoons may have more money, and the young physician's house, automobile, and jewelry may never be as grand as theirs. Yet if physicians approach medicine rightly, they can accumulate wealth of another kind. They can invest their life not in the accumulation of money, but in the promotion of human wholeness. They will have the opportunity to care for people in some of the most poignant moments of human life: birth and death, decay and regeneration, suffering and triumph. They will be called upon every day of their professional lives to develop and display some of the most shining excellences of human character: wisdom, self-control, courage, compassion, and generosity. More than most professions in our culture, medicine offers the opportunity to flourish in profound and enduring ways, by devoting ourselves to the care of something larger than ourselves.

If physicians and other health professionals are to seize fully the opportunity that our teachers, medical schools, the profession of medicine, and our society have bestowed upon us, then we must carefully tend our endowment. Only if we correctly understand what we have been given will we be able to make the most of it. If we allow ourselves to treat our patients as malfunctioning devices, to expend all our energy increasing clinical throughput at the expense of our professional missions as scientists and teachers, or to think more about the money we are earning than the patients we are serving, then we will have squandered our inheritance. On the other hand, if we are to make the most of it, we must correctly understand what we are attempting to do and the role our knowledge and experience should play in helping us to get it done. Consider three different images of our professional endowment.

The first image of our professional endowment is that of a piece of modeling clay. If we are trying to make good use of a piece of modeling clay, what do we need to do? Anyone who has ever worked with modeling clay knows that at first the clay is cold, hard, and intractable. You can't do anything with it until you pick it up and start kneading it, softening it, making it supple. The more you work with it, the better it gets, while the more you keep it idle, the stiffer and less useful it becomes. Like a piece of clay, the human mind can retain impressions, and the more impressions we have made on it, the better at being impressed it becomes. Knowledge is not a static thing, but a dynamic thing. There is no limit to what we can know, except our own cognitive aspirations. There never comes a point at which learning one more thing means we have to forget something else. The size of our understanding is not fixed. In fact, the more we put into it, the more it can hold.

If we are to keep realizing our full potential to understand, we must keep kneading what we see and experience, massaging it and molding it, turning it over and over in our minds, and sharing it with others. The impressions that new knowledge and experiences make on us are a direct product of the knowledge and experiences we have already had. When we read an essay, we pick up on some parts and miss others. Some aspects we find intriguing, others nonsensical. Some aspects make a deep impression, while others don't even register. Like a lump of clay, our ability to retain impressions hinges on how frequently and how deeply we have been impressed in the past. If we go through life with eyes half closed, sleepwalking, then we shouldn't be surprised that nothing makes much of an impression on us or that our lives end up seeming superficial.

There is another reason that remaining supple and adaptable is crucial. Knowledge is not a static thing. The organization and finance of healthcare is not a static thing. The panoply of people and human stories physicians encounter is not a static thing. None of us can stop learning today and expect to do a good job tomorrow. Over a career, the practice of medicine is less the application of what we have been taught and more the search for knowledge spurred by challenges we meet through our patients. What we have learned is important not only because we need to know it to get the job done, but also because it determines what we are capable of recognizing we don't know and how good we become at learning more. Like a piece of clay, putting ourselves to good use means remaining supple and adaptable, seeking out new impressions.

Learning is not the mere accretion of facts, each one giving us one more than we had before. Sometimes adding one more idea means that we must begin anew, re-examining and perhaps even discarding some of the things we supposed we knew. In order to retain some impressions, we must flatten the lump of clay and start over again from scratch. We need to keep critically examining what we think we know in light of new perspectives. Inevitably, we bring some misconceptions and blind spots to our professional activities. If we don't remain open to the possibility that we don't know everything, that we probably harbor some erroneous assumptions, and that others could teach us a thing or two, then we will become hard like unworked clay, and our promise as health professionals will not be realized. The evidence that we are flourishing as professionals and human beings is not merely the diplomas lining our walls, the sum total of what we learned over years in school, but the observations we made and the notes we wrote today, even what we are thinking right now. We must never rest for long on our laurels, for to rest is to begin to grow cold and stiff and lifeless.

The second image of our professional endowment is that of thread. We might think of a physician's spheres of thought and work as strands of thread. For example, one essential thread of medicine is that of biological science, and especially our pursuit of knowledge about the structure and function of the human body. The thread of science, in turn, is made up of many smaller threads, including not only anatomy and physiology, but pathology, microbiology, molecular biology, and so on. Similarly, another major thread of medicine is clinical practice, which is made up of the smaller threads of the various clinical subspecialties, such as internal medicine, surgery, pediatrics, and so on. Clinical practice represents the effort to apply our understanding of biological science to the prevention and treatment of disease. In medical school, we began with the thread of human structure and followed it from the gross dissection laboratory down through organs and tissues, through cells and subcellular organelles to the submicroscopic architecture of individual molecules. We have been privileged to glimpse wonders and beauties of the human organism that most human beings never know.

There are other threads in medicine as well. Beyond the scientific and the clinical threads, there is the thread of medicine's artful side. It is not enough merely to know how cells and organs work or even to have an extensive knowledge of how to diagnose and treat particular diseases. We must also know how to apply that knowledge to the care of real patients, each with a unique biography and worldview. The good physician is more than a mere body mechanic or a biological technician. The good physician is also an artist, who must seek out and help to foster wholeness within the context of a particular patient's life. The physician must know not only how to dissect, titrate, and electrophorese. The physician must also know how to listen, to read between the lines, and to situate the patient's affliction within a larger social and even cosmological context. One patient may experience disease largely as the malfunction of a defective part, such as a stiffened heart valve, while another may experience the same disease as a personal and metaphysical crisis, perhaps raising even religious issues of sin and guilt. The physician must know not only what disease looks like under the microscope, but what it looks like through the lens of a diary.

One of the greatest pitfalls to which we are subject during our professional careers is the temptation to keep the multiple threads of our lives separate and apart. So many forces conspire to fragment our lives, to keep the threads running in parallel, at significant distance from one another. The curricula of our medical schools frequently encourage us to separate the scientific from the humanistic by rarely mentioning them on the same page, or even in the same book. The conventions of the consulting room encourage us to separate the professional from the personal, so we end up checking our lives as human beings, members of families and communities, at the hospital door. Perhaps most egregiously, we keep separate the private and shared threads of our experience. We hold back from allowing our experiences to enrich the lives of others at the very moment that we prevent ourselves from learning from them. Because they are never spoken of in our classes, our consultation rooms, or the corridors of the hospital, we erroneously suppose that such aspects of our lives as love and religion should be kept apart from our professional activities, as though there were some danger of cross-contamination.

But in fact, anyone who has ever woven cloth knows that keeping the fibers in a parallel orientation is a prescription for failure. When all the threads run in parallel, nothing except their individual tension holds them together. To prevent our personal and professional experiences from simply falling through the gaps, we would need to put the threads of biological science, clinical practice, the humane arts, and our personal life experiences and aspirations under such tremendous tension that they would be in constant danger of snapping apart. Some physicians spend significant portions of life in precisely this condition, so tightly strung that each new challenge threatens to undo them. The temptation to keep the threads separate—to compartmentalize our personal lives from our professional lives, to compartmentalize our duties as physicians from our responsibilities as parents and citizens, to compartmentalize our pursuit of health from our religious convictions and life philosophies—compromises our ability to hold on to what we see, experience, and do. If the threads run in parallel, they cannot support one another. As a result, we cannot hold on to much, and too much of life slips right through our grasp.

If we are to develop the capacity to support and hold on to more of our lives, we must interweave the many threads that make them up. We need to bring them into dynamic relation with one another, crisscrossing and interlinking our ideas, experiences, and relationships. We should take pride not in our ability to keep the various spheres of our lives separate, but in the degree to which they are interpenetrated and make up a coherent whole. We should think of ourselves as weavers, creating the most robust and beautiful tapestry of which we are capable. To keep the threads separate is to make ourselves weak, unable to support the moments of real gravity we encounter in personal and professional life. Yet merely combining the threads in a jumble is no better. Instead, we need to combine them as artfully as we can, seeking out and challenging ourselves with the greatest truths we can discover—glimpses of a higher reality that lies around us, if only we have the will and imagination to see.

We should strive to live not as passive recipients of events, but as cocreators of our own existence, the sensitivity, creativity, and courage of which profoundly shape the depth of our experience. Life is a kind of *poesis,* a Greek word that means "making" and provides the basis for our word "poetry." As a poet weaves words together to illuminate beauty and truth, so we can reveal beauty and wisdom for ourselves, our colleagues, and our patients, if only we weave well.

How can we prepare ourselves for such a mission? One strategy is to write every day, or as often as we can. We can write letters, keep a journal, compose poetry or essays. It is in writing, in sitting down and attempting to synthesize diverse elements of our experience, that many of us find the sort of coherence we are seeking. How can we know what we think until we read what we write? We can accomplish much the same objective by telling stories. We can make a point of sharing what we have experienced and done every day and make a point of trying to think through, with the people involved, what it means.

To bring this *poesis,* this weaving, to fruition requires several things. First, we need multiple threads to weave. A one-dimensional life is an impoverished life. Second, we need to allow our experience to inspire us in knitting them together. Each day is an opportunity to explore how the threads of our lives can be more richly interwoven. Finally, we need to cherish the opportunity to lead integrated and coherent lives. Our lives are brief. In thinking of ourselves as poets and weavers, we are also describing what this book aspires to become: a tapestry that weaves together diverse aspects of what it means to be a good professional and a generous human being.

The third and final image of our professional endowment is that of a piece of paper and pencil. There is a story told about a group of newspaper reporters who went out to a fine European restaurant while covering the Olympics some years ago. They were having a good time and the wine was flowing freely. As the night went on, they continued ordering more bottles of the best wine, each one sensing that they might be accumulating quite a tab, but not wanting to appear cheap in the eyes of others. Finally, in the early hours of the morning, their waiter brought them the check, which totaled approximately twenty thousand dollars. The festive mood immediately turned somber, and they sat there ashen-faced, each knowing that no one could afford to pay. As they glanced nervously at each other, an elderly, bald man at an adjacent table motioned the waiter over to him. He took the waiter's pen, and hurriedly scribbled something down on a fresh napkin. The waiter picked up the napkin, studied it for a minute, then came back to the reporters' table and informed them that their bill had been taken care of. Relieved but amazed, they asked the waiter who the gentleman was and how he had taken care of their check. To their surprise, they learned that he was Pablo Picasso. Picasso's hasty sketch on a napkin had more than paid their bill.

The point of the story is that ordinary, everyday things have hidden potential. In the right hands, an ordinary napkin can be transformed into a sublime work of art. In our professional lives, we are given extraordinary opportunities to help reveal beauty and significance in human life, but too often we don't even recognize them. If human lives are like tapestries in the making, then every patient a physician cares for presents a remarkable opportunity. In the course of providing good medical care, a great physician and extraordinary human being could probably find opportunities to learn something important from every patient and at the same time enrich each patient's life.

Some of us deal on an almost daily basis with severely disabled children, whose lives seem at first glance stunted and barren. These are children who will never dress, feed themselves, talk, or perhaps even understand what is said to them. Remarkably, some of these severely disabled children have been adopted by loving families, and some particularly remarkable families have adopted several such children. Most people would prefer not even to look at these children, let alone take them into their homes and care for them around the clock for the rest of their lives. Why do these people do it? If we give ourselves the chance to get to know such families, we realize that some of them are leading extraordinary, almost saintly lives, devoted to nurturing human life in what seems to be its most barren and hopeless circumstances. These people evince the belief that even seemingly hopeless lives are worth preserving and nurturing. A saint has been defined as someone who makes it easier to believe in God. Unless we stop sleepwalking through life with eyes half closed, we will fail to recognize that we are regularly rubbing elbows with saints.

What can each of us do with a blank piece of paper? The growing workload, the accelerating pace, the increasing complexity and sophistication—all these factors in contemporary medicine threaten to prevent us from investing ourselves in caring for patients. It sometimes seems that we no longer have time in medicine even to think, let alone create. When medicine isn't bombarding us with information, our personal lives take up the slack, with a steady barrage of box scores, stock quotes, weather reports, celebrity gossip, and events of the day. We are always busy, the world too much with us. We have become afraid of silence, afraid of a blank piece of paper, anxious perhaps that the temporary calm around us might unmask the void within. T. S. Eliot wrote, "Where is the wisdom we have lost in knowledge; where is the knowledge we have lost in information?" To borrow another image from Eliot, we are in danger of becoming hollow men, hollow physicians, who bring no human insight to our encounters with patients.

The blank piece of paper symbolizes our opportunity to create, to help something beautiful, true, and meaningful take shape in the lives of our patients. If that is our goal, then we must play the role of artists, not mere observers who stand by waiting for something to happen. Frequently, patients and families are too overwhelmed with the sophistication and intensity of contemporary healthcare, not to mention the distress of illness, to realize this potential by themselves. When people are sick and afraid, they need a guide, someone who has seen it before, who knows how these things go, to help them remain open to the larger meanings implicit in our experience.

We must be willing to invest ourselves in our life's work, and avoid leading a life in which nothing of ourselves or our highest aspirations shines through. If we died and our children took the time to examine our work, would they know why we had done it? Would they know who we were? What would they see on the sketchpad of our lives?

Aristotle writes in his *Nicomachean Ethics* that art completes what nature is not able to bring to a finish. A good artist is able to show us things in the world around us that we might otherwise overlook, revealing its full integrity, interconnectedness, and clarity. To reveal that beauty and meaning, the artist must first see it, and to see it, the artist must approach the world from a creative perspective. Whether in art, science, or literature, the world offers up its secrets only to prepared minds. So, too, in medicine, we get out of our patient encounters, our careers, and our lives only what we bring to them. Like the artist, our goal at every moment should be to bring to them and to get out of them as much as we possibly can. We have been given more than we deserve, that is for certain. The question is: What are we going to do with it?

Our mission is not to clutch our endowment to our chests, but to put it to use—not to save it for some rainy day, but to extend it, put it to work, and exert it even to the point of wearing it out. We begin anew every day when we apply what we know to the care of patients, create new knowledge in the laboratory, or teach the wonders of our craft to the next generation of physicians. We get out of it what we bring to it; whoever has will receive more.

What do we bring to this new beginning? To those who bring little—who don't keep kneading the clay of their understanding, interweaving the diverse perspectives of medical practice, and sketching out new visions of medicine's possibilities for themselves and their patients—little will be given. They will live out their days half awake, percussing chests, drafting prescriptions, and earning a better-than-decent living, but never learning anything from their patients and never giving back to their patients anything more than what every customer has a right to expect. On the other hand, for those who approach medicine with the eye of an artist—developing their curiosity, honing their capacities for creativity, and deepening their passion for coherence—great rewards are in store. The precise shape and pattern and vision they will take, however, are as yet unknown. The precise shape and pattern and vision they will take are left for each of us to discover and bring to life.

13

HOARDING AND SHARING

Matthew 19, Mark 10, and Luke 18 each tell essentially the same story. Jesus is approached by a rich young man who asks him what he needs to do to inherit eternal life. Jesus responds that he should keep the commandments, sell his possessions and give the money to the poor, and then come and follow him. Because of his great wealth, we are told, the young man cannot comply. At which point Jesus turns to his followers and says, "I tell you the truth, it is hard for a rich man to enter the kingdom of heaven. Again I tell you, it is easier for a camel to go through the eye of a needle than for a rich man to enter the kingdom of God." Why does Jesus choose this metaphor, and what does it say about the relationship between wealth and human goodness?

One popular interpretation is that Jesus was referring to a gate into Jerusalem that had been nicknamed "the eye of the needle." The gate had been constructed with a low ceiling, so that a camel could pass through only in a kneeling posture, which would require that the camel's baggage be unloaded first. The implication would be that rich people must first unburden themselves of their own baggage, their wealth, before they can find true goodness. Unfortunately for this interpretation, there is no historical evidence that such a gate ever existed. Another interpretation suggests that the Greek word *kamilos* should actually be *kamêlos,* which means "rope." On this interpretation, it is harder for a rich person to enter the kingdom of God than to pass a rope through the eye of a needle. Also, the word for camel in Aramaic, the language in which Jesus spoke, is *gamla,* which also means "rope," perhaps because ropes were made of camel hair.

Yet there is no reason not to take the story at face value; namely, that Jesus truly intends his followers to consider the impossibility of passing a camel through the eye of a needle. Why this particular metaphor? For one thing, the eye of a needle called to mind an extremely small space. In an era before microscopes and atomic theory, the eye of a needle may have been the smallest imaginable opening, so small that threading even a single fiber through it can prove devilishly difficult. Moreover, in the land of Jesus, the camel would have been the largest animal that people encountered with any regularity. Jesus' suggestion that riches are somehow inimical to goodness flies in the face of the popular teaching of the day, which held that prosperity was a sign of blessedness. In the books of Leviticus, Deuteronomy, and Proverbs, wealth is often cited as one of the rewards God bestows on the righteous.

What is so problematic about wealth? According to the Bible story, part of the answer lies in the difficulty we have in parting with it, a difficulty that is not difficult to understand. If we have labored a good part of our lives to acquire wealth, then we have a great deal invested in it. It is likely to be an important part of our self-image, our sense of who we are. It is also a sign of our success in the eyes of others, an obvious way of keeping score. How well are we doing in life, and how well have we done? According to the "prosperity equals excellence" model, we can answer this question by measuring our net worth, counting up the number of dollars we have to our name. Even wealth that is not earned but inherited may still seem a familial trust, which we are responsible for handing on in good order to the next generation. Wealth means security, prestige, and freedom, including both the ability to get what we want and the capacity to help others. What would it mean to our family members if we gave away every cent?

Yet there are senses in which, far from liberating us, wealth can be a prison. The more of our time and attention it consumes, and the greater the role it plays in our lives, the more likely we are to find ourselves enslaved to it. What do we see when we look in the mirror? If the answer is restricted to the businesses we have built, the investment portfolios we have assembled, or the expensive possessions we have accumulated, then there is a distinct danger that we have become mere mercenaries. Mercenary comes from the same Latin root as the word "merchant," *merces,* which means "wages" or "price." A mercenary is someone who is motivated by the desire for money or other material gain. Mercenaries can be bought, because they always have their price. When we realize that we cannot bear to part with our money, we have joined their ranks.

When we cannot live without our wealth, we have become its prisoners. We have adopted a system of priorities in life that puts money first and other goods second. We have fallen into the trap of greed, the very antithesis of true prosperity. In his *Nicomachean Ethics,* Aristotle suggests that allowing wealth to ensnare us is not only morally perilous but also rationally unsound. Wealth, he argues, is not an end in itself, but a mere means to other ends. We want money not for its own sake, but because of what we can get with it. If we begin to think of money as an end in itself, then our priorities in life have fallen seriously out of order. We have mistaken the means for the end and thereby consigned ourselves to a life of deep discontent. If merely accumulating more money is our life's goal, it becomes impossible to say when we have enough.

If we can never say that we have enough of something, we can never be happy with what we have. If one million dollars is good, then two million dollars is better, and three million dollars better still. Why do people who have devoted their whole lives to making money find it out of character to say that they have enough? Because it requires them to identify some new good other than money to which they can now turn their attention. The insatiable appetite for more is fueled by comparison with others. No sooner do we reach whatever goal we have in mind than we become aware of someone else who has more. So long as someone else has more than we do, we cannot be content. Each time we are surpassed by someone else, it only further incites our envy and greed.

In Moliere's *The Miser,* the character of Harpagon represents greed reduced to absurdity. When this prototypical skinflint realizes that his beloved strongbox is missing and has likely been stolen, he cries out, "They've cut my throat! They've stolen my money! Won't somebody bring me back to life by restoring my money?" There is something farcical and amusing about the miser, but underneath he is deeply tragic. His greed threatens to destroy everyone around him, including those closest to him. Harpagon is so determined to keep his deceased wife's inheritance for himself that when an acquaintance compliments him on his health by telling him, "You will bury your children and your grandchildren," his response is marked by obvious delight. So voracious is his greed that it consumes even his love for his children.

Being wealthy, and especially devoting our lifetimes to acquiring more wealth, tends to distract us from what is most worth living for, fixing our attention on less important things. When we see our lives in such terms, giving and sharing become difficult, incomprehensible, even perverse. Why should we give or share what we have when doing so only reduces our wealth, thereby diminishing our happiness and, it seems, making us smaller? On such terms, opening up our hands, lending a hand, and passing on what we hold to others simply does not make sense. By contrast, nothing seems more natural than grasping at what others have, and once we have gotten hold of it, clutching it tightly. We begin to see the world around us and the people who populate it as resources to be exploited, perhaps even plundered.

Wealth becomes a force that divides us, even setting us at one another's throats. At its best, competition can spur us to greater effort and bring out the best in us. As athletes, students, artists, and entrepreneurs, competition challenges us to do better. It stimulates innovation and can raise everyone's level of performance. When it does, we all benefit. At its worst, however, competition can prove profoundly destructive. It may lead to a zero-sum mentality, in which one person's victory seems to require another person's loss and gaining more for ourselves forces someone else to make do with less. When we think of wealth in these terms, the flourishing of others seems threatening. Soon we wish others ill. We would sooner possess little yet more than everyone else than a great deal but least of all.

Wealth can divide us in other ways as well. The economist Thorstein Veblen introduced the term "conspicuous consumption" to describe goods and services purchased primarily to display wealth and not out of any material need. A related term is "invidious consumption," those goods and services we consume with the intention of inciting a sense of envy in others. As in a game of chess, where one player's victory requires another player's loss, we find ourselves in a zero-sum situation. When one person buys a luxury automobile, expensive jewelry, or a posh vacation home, another person can either concede the game of status seeking or go out and buy an item of greater value. Gated communities can be attractive for a similar reason, because they enable prosperous homeowners to feel set apart and special compared to their less affluent fellow citizens.

The counterpart of conspicuous consumption is conspicuous giving. Unable to achieve the desired level of status or envy merely by purchasing goods or services, we turn to ostentation in giving as a way of showing off our wealth. By giving to someone else, we demonstrate that we have more than they do. In so doing, we seek to shore up our own sense of self-worth, trying to make ourselves feel superior. We think our ability to give makes us somehow better than the person or people to whom we are giving. Such judgments are inherently divisive since they accentuate the separation of the giver from the receiver.

Yet giving need not divide us. It can, in fact, bring us closer together. This is what true generosity aims at. We can be shaped not only by getting, spending, and giving in the conspicuous sense. We can also shape ourselves and others by giving that fosters a shared sense of hope and compassion, as well as mutual understanding. Such gifts actually build community, drawing our attention not to the ways we differ from one another, but the ways we are fundamentally alike. On this account, wealth turns out to be a relatively superficial aspect of our identity, not unlike the clothes we wear. There is no question that our economic status exerts an important effect on who we are, but underneath are deeper and more fundamental attributes.

The highest possibilities for the development of human character do not lie in separating ourselves from one another. They lie in integrating ourselves with others through friendships, family, and community. We can act in a truly courageous fashion only when we are so dedicated to a particular person or group of people that we are prepared to lay down our lives on their behalf. We can act in a truly generous fashion only when we recognize the good of promoting the flourishing of others. Separation diminishes us, while awareness of our mutual interconnectedness and interdependence opens up new opportunities for flourishing. To look at another person and see only impoverishment is to perceive with a constricted sense of generosity. To see instead a human being just like ourselves, albeit one who happens to be in greater need, is to experience the liberation of our generative potential.

One of the most philanthropically debilitating notions is that of the self-made person. Some of us mistakenly suppose that we are completely responsible for our own fates, that we have picked ourselves up entirely by our own bootstraps, that we do not owe anything to anyone. The humbler the circumstances from which we began and the higher we have risen above them, the more inclined we seem to be to fall into this trap. Yet none of us, even those of us with the most remarkable rags-to-riches stories, is truly a self-made human being. Even those of us who did not inherit any wealth enjoy an immense legacy. Each of us acceded to rich language and categories of thought, a treasure trove of folklore and culture, and technological marvels of which our ancestors could not have dreamed.

In thinking about my own career in medicine, it would be easy for me to think of myself as a self-made physician. After all, I worked hard to gain admission to medical school, spent nine years in medical school, residency, and fellowship training learning my craft, and poured myself since into the pursuit of excellence. Whatever benefits I enjoy as a physician—whether income, status, or satisfaction—must be wholly mine, since I was the one who earned them. Yet if I see anything at all in medicine, it is because I am perched on the shoulders of giants. Much more intelligent, creative, and dedicated people went before me. It is in their blood, sweat, and tears that our contemporary textbooks were written.

Instead of thinking of ourselves as self-made physicians, my colleagues and I should call to mind the immense debt we owe the great and even not-so-great healers who came before us. When new patients entrust themselves to our care, they do so not because we have earned that trust, but because others who came before us did. The knowledge and skills we rely on to diagnose and treat their conditions were not our discovery. In virtually every case, they were taught to us by someone else, who in turn learned them from someone else.

Medicine is not personal property, something that anyone can own. Instead, it is a trust. We act on its behalf not as owners but as stewards, like priests guarding a flame. Our mission is not to burn it up, but to pass it on, hopefully blazing a bit more brightly than the day it was handed to us.

The metaphor of a torch is illuminating. There is an ancient saying that a single torch can light thousands of others, yet the life of the torch is not shortened. When we pass on understanding, such as the knowledge and skills of a contemporary physician, we do not diminish our own fund of knowledge. If anything, we tend to augment it, for in teaching it to others we gain a deeper understanding ourselves. Knowledge is not a zero-sum good. It is not diminished through sharing. Generally speaking, it is a positive-sum good, which is actually augmented through sharing. When we share with others what we know, we end up with more than we began with. In sharing freely what we have, we gain a better understanding of the abundance we work and live with all the time.

Even in the realm of material wealth, the zero-sum mentality is inadequate. Except by resorting to crime, no one will ever become wealthy, or even earn a living, by taking from other people. Our economic system is built on exchange, and for people to exchange freely implies that each has something the other wants. In a pure exchange economy, people will not part with what they have unless they can get something better through the transaction. Hence the way to get rich is not by taking from other people, but by helping them to get what they need and want. We must think first not of our own advantage, but of what we can do for others. Most of all, we must think of the mutual benefit we can derive from sharing with one another what each of us has to offer. Diversity is crucial, because if we were exactly the same in every respect, we would not benefit nearly as much as we do by pooling our diverse interests and abilities.

So long as we operate from a perspective of scarcity, giving is stunted. It is difficult to give away tangible goods such as food, clothing, and shelter when we feel we do not have enough for ourselves. Even intangible goods, such as time and attention, are difficult to share when we believe that our own needs in these areas are poorly met. Because scarcity so undermines generosity, it is vital that we cultivate a shared sense of abundance, even blessedness. The Greek word *eudaimonia*, usually translated as "happiness," may also be rendered as "blessedness." Those who have counted their blessings, who are most fully aware of the blessings they enjoy in life, are best endowed to share what they have with others.

Such self-consciously blessed people need be neither the most materially prosperous nor the most naturally gifted. Often the most generous among us turn out to be people of relatively modest means. What they lack in wealth they make up through a deep understanding of those they help and a dedication to making a difference in their lives. This kind of philanthropic activity is within the reach of every single person, even the least among us. None of us lacks the means to be generous. We can give not only from our wallets, but also from our hearts. Each of us has an equal amount of time every day, and there is always time enough to give to someone in need. We can always lend a compassionate ear or a helping hand. We can let someone know that we believe in them more than they believe in themselves. Even in receiving, we can be generous.

The mere fact that we are being compensated for our efforts need not diminish the worth of what we are contributing. Consider, for example, an outstanding teacher. Such a person is paid to come to work every day and might not be able to continue to do so without the income and benefits the position provides. Yet in the course of fulfilling the formal requirements of the job, a truly generous teacher may go far beyond the call of duty. Great teachers give more of themselves than the job requires. They genuinely care about their students, and this opens up opportunities to make a real difference in the lives of students, families, colleagues, and communities. Their excellence is a form of supererogation, paying more than is owed. As such, they embody true generosity.

This explains why personal generosity and the "output" of the philanthropic sector can never be measured strictly in dollars. We can measure the number of dollars people give and the number of hours they volunteer, but we cannot measure their dedication to excellence. We need to take into account not only the quantity of product we produce, but also the quality of the work we do. There are ways of helping people that diminish them and ways of helping that enrich them. In some situations, treating someone respectfully or kindly may be just as important, perhaps even more important, than the amount of money that changes hands.

14

LESSONS FROM THE LEAST

Some of us prefer to avoid people with disabilities. When we see a man or a woman whose twisted posture, slurred speech, or shuddering gait suggests mental retardation or cerebral palsy, our impulse is to turn the other way. There is something about deformity that makes many of us wince, like hearing a beloved musical composition played off key. It is offputting, jarring, unseemly. Hence we segregate our communities so that we encounter people with severe disabilities only rarely, if at all. Most of the time, we do not mind forgetting that the least among us even exist.

I know a man who regards this attitude as profoundly mistaken. His name is John. For five years, John has participated in a residential program that provides care for 240 adults with severe disabilities. Each week he works two twenty-four-hour shifts, literally living with a small group of "clients." Originally he did this as a volunteer. Now he gets paid, though not particularly well. John is part of a larger team that includes nurses, physicians, physical and occupational therapists, social workers, administrators, and behavioral consultants. Caring for the disabled is not a money-making proposition, and despite support from Social Security and Medicaid, the program in which John participates runs a multimillion-dollar deficit each year.

People who try John's line of work soon realize that caring for the disabled requires them to march to the beat of a different drummer. Many of the clients need adaptive tools to carry out even the simplest tasks, such as feeding themselves and combing their hair. One man requires two hours each morning just to get out of bed, shower, brush his teeth, and get dressed. When you walk through a shopping mall or a museum with a group of disabled persons, some people merely avoid you. Others look at you with disdain or even disgust, as though you are ruining their day. Life with disability is not a cakewalk. Yet John believes that caring for people with severe disabilities offers many rewards.

He reports that he has found unexpected serenity in the enjoyment of simple things. To his clients, seemingly insignificant events often spark great enthusiasm. Each Sunday after attending religious services, John takes his group to a local grocery store, where each client buys a soda pop from the vending machine. To most of us, such an outing would seem trivial. To John's group, however, it is a major event that everyone eagerly anticipates throughout the week. He recalls a physically impaired client whose face lit up like the sun when they discussed the possibility that he might be able to obtain a driver's license. John's clients reawaken our sense of wonder at everyday life.

Contact with the disabled offers glimpses of our humanity. Differences in our cultural backgrounds, levels of educational attainment, stations in life, and even physical or mental abilities cannot mask the common alloy at the core of us all. Everyone, even the richest and most famous, needs to get out of bed in the morning, get dressed, use the toilet, and eat. Everyone, no matter how humble their circumstances, needs food, shelter, and medical care. Everyone, no matter what their intelligence level, needs to love and be loved. John's clients are not impressed by how much money people make, how often their names appear in the newspaper, or how many degrees they hold. They are, however, impressed by friendliness and good cheer. John says that their simplicity mirrors the divine benevolence that makes the sun shine on everyone alike.

John's clients have hopes and insecurities just like the rest of us. One day soon after John began his work with the disabled, he took his group on an outing to a local bowling alley. As they entered the facility, one client lingered at the window. A bystander might have assumed that the poor fellow was afraid to enter. From the way the man gazed steadily into the window and turned his head from side to side, however, John realized that he was inspecting his reflection. As John approached, the man turned to him and asked, "How's my hair look?" To be human is to care about how we appear in the eyes of others. From that moment forward, John knew that his clients are fundamentally no different from the rest of us.

John learned another lesson that day. While they were bowling, a woman walked up to him and admitted in a whisper that she had always been afraid to try to talk to people who are "like that." She nodded toward one of the clients and in a low voice asked John, "Does he like candy bars?" John politely urged her to ask the man herself. She paused for a moment, then walked over to the man and asked in a loud voice, "DO . . . YOU . . . LIKE . . . CANDY . . . BARS?" One of the top priorities of John's program is to get disabled adults out of the institutional setting and into the community, where they can interact with "normal" people. Often it is not the clients but the "normal" people who are in most urgent need of socialization.

John finds that when people in the community get to meet and interact with members of his group, many of the old stereotypes and misconceptions melt away. We learn that disabled does not necessarily mean stupid. We cannot necessarily gauge by mathematical ability how friendly a person will be. Fairness and honesty are not necessarily correlated with IQ. And there is no guarantee that a large vocabulary will be accompanied by a compassionate heart. When we work and play with the disabled, we discover many opportunities to have fun together, if only our heart is in it. There is something infectious about sincere joy, and that is one thing that John's clients are able to dispense in abundance. Says John: "Anyone with half a heart can't help but grow inside when they see those big smiles."

Caring for people with disabilities provides deep insights on dealing with adversity. If anyone has cause to feel they were dealt a bad hand in life, it is John's clients. Because of the way they look, move, and speak, most people shun them. Things the rest of us can do without even thinking, such as tying our shoes, require major effort on their part. Sometimes, despite their best efforts, they fail anyway. There is much that they do not understand, and the sublimities of human drama and art are forever lost to many of them. Yet they rarely complain. They take setbacks in stride. They do not waste their time wallowing in self-pity. Never in five years has John heard one of his clients say, "My life is horrible" or "I wish I had not been born."

A cynic might respond, "Of course not! They do not complain because they lack insight. They are just so dimwitted that they are incapable of recognizing the depth of their misery." In John's view, however, they are not stupid, but plain and simple, two traits from which we could learn some valuable lessons. They do not occupy themselves with denying who and what they are or pretending to be something they are not. They are not lost in the labyrinth of their own fantasies, replaying their past mistakes and wondering what might have been. Instead, they make a sincere effort to lead the life they have been given. Though some would say it is not enough, they rejoice in life as they know it, and in that rejoicing put some "normal" people to shame.

An especially noteworthy feature of John's clients is their innocence. In order to supplement his income, John has recently commenced a training program to become a sheriff's deputy. Though he has only a few months under his belt, he has already begun to appreciate how cynical law enforcement could make a person. Evidently, many of us in the general public think nothing of lying to law enforcement officers should it suit our interests to do so. By contrast, John's clients are utterly guileless. If they break something, they admit it. If they want something, they ask for it. If they offend someone, they feel heartily sorry for it. Mendacity is simply not a part of their nature. They manifest a childlike trust and faith in others that renders deception unthinkable. Why should they deny what is, or assert what is not? As a disabled child once intimated to me, "Why should I try to cover it up? Would the truth change because I tried to hide it?"

Despite ample reason to be angry and resentful, the members of John's group exhibit a deep capacity to forgive. Some of them have been all but abandoned by their families. Many never see their parents or siblings. They may receive one phone call a year, if they are lucky. Years ago, when their families first decided that they could not care for them at home, some were sent to state institutions where they fell victim to physical and mental abuse. All have been taunted and ridiculed because of their disabilities. John has even seen some of his colleagues treat clients as though they were not really there, talking down to them in demeaning and sometimes frankly cruel ways. In five years, however, John has never observed a client hold a grudge.

Some people point out that the members of John's group are not productive. Because of their limited capabilities, they generate little in the way of goods or services. Moreover, their care consumes resources that some believe could be put to better use. "Why should we keep spending money to provide nice lives for disabled people, when they will never be able to give back to society?" they ask. "Wouldn't we accomplish more by spending that money on normal people?" John regards such questions as a sign of confusion. In posing them, we mistake dependency for worthlessness. John responds to such questions with questions of his own: Are we prepared to say that every person who does not pull his or her own weight should be cast off from society, or granted only the minimum subsidy necessary to sustain life? Where would we draw the line between people who are "normal" enough to receive aid and those who are so abnormal that we can comfortably ignore them?

John points out that the line between normal and abnormal, between whole and defective, is not fixed. The way we sort people today may not be the way we will sort them tomorrow. Any of us could discover at any moment that fate has moved us or someone we love from one side of that line to the other. Not all of John's clients were born the way they are today. Some were once very successful people who suffered head trauma in motor vehicle accidents, or developed brain tumors, or suffered strokes. Without warning, they suddenly found themselves severely disabled for the rest of their lives.

John thinks of our parents, siblings, spouses, and children. What would happen if a catastrophe left them in a state of extreme dependency? Would we seize the first opportunity to cast them off? What would our response reveal about who we are and what we hold dear in life? John hopes that if such a situation ever befell his family, they would be cared for by someone as compassionate as he has tried to be. He shudders at the thought that someone would look at his mother, his father, or his brothers and sisters and say, "These people are worthless. We should get rid of them." Instead, we need to remember some things. First, we need to remember that every person with a disability *is* someone's son or daughter, sister or brother. Second, we need to recall that the mere fact that people are disabled does not make them any less human. Finally, we need to recognize that there is much to be learned from the disabled and much joy to be found in their company.

Disability and disrepute are linked, but they are linked less through the stunted abilities of the disabled than by the limitations of our moral imagination. Morally speaking, the inability of some people to provide for themselves is less problematic than our own reluctance to share with those in need. We need to open our eyes and see anew. We need to rediscover our sense of wonder that life comes in many forms. Compared to the world we know, a world populated by only perfect people would be a less colorful, rich, and engaging place.

A perfect world populated by only perfect people would be a world without compassion, the very possibility of which arises from our capacity to suffer. It would be a world without hope, which is grounded in the possibility that we could become better than we are. Even our capacity for wisdom would be diminished. There is great wisdom in the ability to peer below a person's warped exterior and appreciate the beauty of the human spirit that lies beneath. If we open our eyes to the least among us, we may even glimpse the most surpassing truth of all: that life in all its forms, no matter how limited, is a miraculous and precious thing.

15

LOWER AND HIGHER

What is the world made of? Various ancient philosophers such as Anaximines and Thales posited a single substance, such as water, air, fire, or earth. Some of their successors, including Aristotle, argued that the world is made up of multiple such elements. More recently, we have expanded this list even further, and today's periodic table of the elements boasts more than a hundred members. If we asked high school students today what makes up the world, they might respond, "atoms." The more sophisticated among them might invoke the constituents of these once seemingly indivisible building blocks, including protons, neutrons, and electrons. Physicists now believe that these subatomic particles are made up of even smaller constituents, including quantum mechanical entities such as quarks.

Is the world made up of such atomic and subatomic particles? It certainly has properties that concepts such as the atom help us to understand. We can explain the density of a material according to the elements of which it is composed, and the concept of electron shells is very useful in understanding why and how different chemicals react with one another. Yet there are other everyday phenomena that seem profoundly non-atomic, in the sense that they are not chemical and not physical. Consider, for example, the phenomenon of generosity. What light do concepts such as ionic bonding and conservation of mass shed on giving? Generosity and other human excellences have no mass, no color, and no location in space. They do not manifest the features of reality recognized by physics and chemistry. Yet they are undeniably real.

To be sure, generosity depends in some ways on chemistry and physics. If we are struck in the head by a sufficiently massive object traveling at a sufficiently high speed, we will not be generous anymore. Likewise, if our biochemical milieu is sufficiently disrupted—say, by a fall in the pH of our blood or the addition of some extra potassium chloride—our capacity for generosity vanishes. Yet to say that a certain set of conditions is necessary—that we need a particular serum pH and potassium concentration—is not to say that we can create life or imbue generosity merely by reproducing such conditions. A person may be perfectly healthy yet utterly indifferent to giving.

Consider a baseball game. On the one hand, every motion in the game, including throwing, batting, catching, and running, can be understood in terms of chemical and physical events. If it were not for the transmission of electrical impulses along the axons of nerves and the action of muscle proteins such as troponin and myosin, the motions of the game would be impossible. Similarly, were Newton's laws of motion somehow suspended, the game could not take place. Both chemists and physicists can describe the action, and the principles they describe are necessary for play to occur. Yet what they describe—the chemist's reactions and the physicist's forces—do not constitute baseball. Their analysis would be essentially the same whether they were describing baseball or some entirely different sport, such as tennis or football, or even no sport at all.

Baseball is both a chemical phenomenon and a physical phenomenon, but it is neither strictly chemical nor strictly physical. To thoroughly understand what transpires on the baseball field, we must repair to additional concepts, which operate at quite different levels. These concepts include the acts of throwing, catching, batting, and running. They also include performing each of them more or less well. The same goes for concepts such as scorekeeping, teamwork, and strategy, which have different meanings in baseball than they do in other sports. At a critical juncture of a baseball game it would make no more sense to leap out of our seats and shout "conservation of momentum!" than "touchdown!" The recognition that we have witnessed a crucial turning point in the game requires a different level of understanding than natural science can provide.

Disputes might arise over which kind of knowledge is more important, the understanding of the natural scientist or that of the baseball enthusiast. Natural scientists could argue that their concepts are much more universal than baseball's, pertaining to all events that occur in the universe. Yet physical laws provide virtually no insight into the distinctive events taking place on a baseball field. They do not help us understand what the players are trying to accomplish and why. They do not enable us to predict what any particular player is likely to do next. A deeper understanding of physical principles may help a player throw or swing more effectively, but physical principles do not explain why anyone would choose to engage in such activities in the first place, or why they are worth doing well.

In baseball, both lower and higher levels of understanding are at work. The lowest or most fundamental levels of understanding, including Newtonian mechanics and biochemistry, apply across the board to a variety of everyday activities, including baseball. However, they do not help us understand the essence of baseball itself. If we know baseball, we operate with a much deeper level of insight and explanatory power about what baseball players, managers, and fans are doing. To be a spectator who understands only the physics would be like watching a baseball game through the eyes of a dog— just as the dog sees every movement of the ball as an invitation to a game of catch, so the pure physicist sees every player's action as just another instance of matter in motion.

The same could be said for any number of fields of human endeavor. The music of a violin, for example, could be understood as nothing more than the vibrations produced by scraping catgut across horse's hair. The sight of a mother nursing her infant baby could be accounted for as the instinct of a biological organism to provide nutrients for its offspring. Generosity could be explained strictly as a type of economic transaction, though perhaps a one-way one. We can always attempt to account for the higher in terms of the lower. Love can be explained in terms of pleasure, and pleasure in terms of health. Likewise, the pursuit of fame can be explained in terms of power, and power in terms of wealth. Yet what do we lose when we attempt to reduce the panoply of human affairs to a mere lust for power or wealth?

We should not expect any one approach to explain everything. The world is a variegated and complex place, and multiple approaches are necessary. No single human discipline has a monopoly on the natural sciences. Chemistry will not completely supplant biology, any more than physics will one day overthrow chemistry. Each has its place in our understanding of the natural world. Likewise, literature, art, religion, and philosophy each has a place among the humanities. None can completely explain away the others. And the natural sciences can no more supplant the humanities than the humanities can supplant the natural sciences. The humanities depend on the natural sciences in the sense that physical and chemical conditions are necessary for art to be created and appreciated. Yet it is to the humanities, not the natural sciences, that we must turn to understand the scientific impulse to know.

To arrive at a comprehensive understanding of the world around us, we need multiple different modes of inquiry. This is as powerful an indicator as any that creation is not solely about us. After all, the world did not begin with us, and it is likely to persist long after we are gone. Perhaps earth and sea are not teeming with life solely for our nourishment. Perhaps the sun does not rise and set solely for our pleasure. Perhaps nature was not made intelligible purely so that we could conquer it. Perhaps the ultimate challenge for human beings is less to remake the world according to our own desires than to seek out the larger patterns of truth in the world and conform our aspirations to them. Our mission is less to drown out the world with the sound of our own whistling than to bring our lives into harmony with the music of creation.

If creation does have higher and lower orders, then our mission is to discern the difference between the higher and lower. While never forsaking the lower, we are challenged to order our lives as much as possible according to the higher. Pleasure is a vital and necessary part of a complete human life, but pleasure is neither the highest nor the best good to which we can aspire. Acting generously is more important than merely having fun. It would be a mistake to confine our giving strictly to those instances where acting generously is also pleasurable. Generosity should not conform to pleasure. Rather, pleasure should conform to generosity. We should so educate our faculty of desire that we learn to take great pleasure in acts of true generosity while learning to feel pain at instances of greed and excessive largesse.

Wealth is a real human good. Without some of the resources

money can buy, it is difficult to flourish as a human being, family, or community. Moreover, people whose level of wealth is above a certain threshold are probably more likely to lead full lives than those below it. Yet we cannot induce a state of flourishing merely by giving people more money, any more than we can make ourselves healthier by simply stuffing ourselves with more food or medicines. Wealth is a real good, but it occupies a relatively low rung on the ladder of human goods. It would be folly to confine our attempts to understand generosity to economics. Giving and receiving money is one of the ways we can be generous, but different and greater opportunities for liberality are open to us.

We are not presented with a choice between wealth and pleasure, wealth and fame, or wealth and generosity. We need not completely forgo any one for the sake of the other. If we are fortunate, it is possible to enjoy all these goods at once. To lead full lives, however, we need to determine the relative worth of each. To which do we want to devote the most time and energy, and with which would we elect to occupy ourselves less? Consider what happens when we dine with friends. At least two goods are involved, the pleasures associated with the food and the pleasures of the conversation. Which is ultimately more satisfying, food or fellowship? Which should we be prepared to subordinate to the other? As Aristotle argued, if we put food first, we are little better than cattle who happen to graze in the same field. We are truer to human nature if we put conversation first.

Biting off a piece of fruit, chewing it up, and swallowing it is not terribly inspiring. Nor is generosity that consists of nothing more than writing a check. We can gain insight into what happens on a baseball field by studying events in terms of mechanical physics, but it is impossible to inspire the players in such terms. To understand what inspires us to give, students of generosity need to look beyond the amount of money that changes hands. Fundraising and managing non-profit organizations are important matters, but they rest on a deeper foundation: the inspiration to give.

What inspires us? Above all, we tend to be inspired by narratives, stories. We are moved to give to people when we see them as part of our story or ourselves as part of their story. For generosity to find expression, an act of giving must fit into a narrative, and that narrative must be one we care about. The story represents the larger whole into which our gift fits as a part, the context of meaning in which giving is situated. Among all the ways we could give, among all the potential beneficiaries, which fit best in the stories about which we care most? Above all, which are the stories about which we sense a calling to care most? In some cases, we may be entirely unaware of these stories. In others, we may perceive them only dimly, as if through a dark glass. So long as we fail to see these larger contexts, our capacity to give will be stunted. Once we do see them, our capacity to give can be fully realized.

Each of us wants to lead a life that is faithful to what is most real and important. If we mistakenly suppose that we are the most important thing in the universe, we cannot but lead superficial and misguided lives. We are like travelers attempting to follow a defective map. What we see never matches our vision of the way things are supposed to be, we regularly feel lost, and we never end up at our intended destination. Our characteristic state in life is one of disorientation, bewilderment, frustration, and even despair. So long as we expect to find fulfillment by making and spending money, life must seem hollow. To reorient ourselves appropriately, we must attend to our internal moral compass. We need to visit and revisit this vital question: What gives us the sense of being most deeply and intensely alive and active?

For most of us, the answer relates to giving and sharing. We feel most intensely alive and active when we are involved in giving of ourselves to others, sharing the best in us with someone else. So long as we think only of ourselves, we live in a kind of prison. At our worst, we become curved in on ourselves, just as space itself curves in on itself in the vicinity of what astrophysicists call a black hole. These incredibly dense and massive objects have a gravitational force so great that even light itself cannot escape them. When we become curved in on ourselves, we see everything in terms of what it means to us, always looking for ways to turn events to our own advantage. Compared to this jail cell of self-preoccupation, giving represents an opportunity for liberation. By sharing with someone else, we can free ourselves from the false idol in the mirror.

An actress tells of the excitement she experienced when, as an adult, she one day discovered her deceased father's diary. She immediately immersed herself in it, enthralled by the sense that the diary would allow her to reconnect with him. By reading it, she could share his impressions of important events in her family's life, such as the day that he and her mother met, their courtship, and their marriage. It quickly occurred to her that she could also look up his reflections on the day she was born, and she quickly turned to that date in the diary. To her disappointment, she found an entry on that date, but it consisted solely of financial matters. The event of her birth was not even mentioned.

Today most of us do not keep journals, but if we did, what events would be sufficient to register with us? What would someone reading our journal make of the entries they found there? Would they find catalogs of our purchases or lists of our grievances? What insights might they glean about our moral compass? What did we care most about? What moved us? For what, if anything, would we have been prepared to lay our lives on the line? What feelings did we inspire in others? Did others regard us with suspicion or resentment, or did we inspire trust and even loyalty and affection? To what degree was the flourishing of others something in which we invested ourselves? To what were we committed, and how did those commitments liberate us to contribute?

The Bible suggests that in order to find ourselves, we must lose ourselves. We most promote our development as human beings not by shielding ourselves and holding ourselves back—conserving what we have for some indefinite future—but by committing ourselves in the service of a higher purpose. When we attempt to understand others, work on behalf of others, and even sacrifice ourselves for others, we most fully realize what and who we are. This is not a paradox or some cruel twist of fate. It is a natural reflection of the fact that there are more important things in the universe, things more worth living for, than each of us. When we see those things for what they are, what we experience is not a sense of endangerment, but a sense of peace. Only then can we trust that we have aligned ourselves appropriately with the larger order of things.

This does not require that we eschew money, fame, or power, any more than we should completely ignore food, shelter, and sleep. But it does imply that the pursuit of wealth is appropriate only when situated in an appropriate higher context. Ideally, we would see our job not primarily as a means of making money, but a means of serving others, of contributing, of making a difference. That we get paid for it is not insignificant, but it is not paramount. Professionals see their work as focused on internal goods, goods intrinsic to the work itself, which would not be affected by an increase or decrease in compensation. For a health professional, such an intrinsic good might be the opportunity to play a part in healing and comforting the sick. For a philanthropist, it might be helping someone acquire an important life skill, such as reading. External goods such as wealth, fame, and power count for something, but the work itself matters most.

When income or prestige predominates, career takes precedence over profession. A careerist would be happy to switch positions if a more lucrative or prestigious offer came along. A professional, too, might accept a different position, but only to do better work, to make a bigger contribution. A professional works for the benefit of others and strives to earn their trust. To be a professional is to profess, to declare publicly, such a commitment. If we have nothing invested in our jobs but our earning power, then we are not professionals. Likewise if we derive nothing from work but income, prestige, or power. Professionals see work not in contractual terms, as something to deliver pending appropriate compensation, but in terms of opportunity, even privilege. A true professional considers it a privilege to serve.

Why do we fear losing our jobs? Is it because we would be unable to make ends meet, or because of a loss of face? No, if we are fortunate, it is primarily because we would have difficulty being ourselves, our best selves, without that work. Far from freeing us up to spend more time in the service of others, losing our jobs would make it more difficult to serve, at least in the way we believe we are meant to. Professionals see in a career a prime opportunity to be generous, to cultivate generosity, and to make a difference in the lives of others. Being compensated for service does not deprive us of the opportunity to be generous, at least not so long as our greatest ambition is to enrich the lives of others.

In discussing generosity, there is a natural tendency to emphasize the actions of the giver. Yet it is no less important to attend to the role of the recipient. In every instance of generosity, both are necessary. Simply to pour cash out of an airplane or throw food off the back of a truck might seem noteworthy, but it would not shine as an act of generosity. In such circumstances, how can givers see and understand those they are intending to help? From their point of view, the recipients are likely to appear nameless and faceless. In the best generosity, giver and recipient need to know one another and to feel drawn into partnership with one another. When generosity is at its best, both feel a calling. The giver feels a calling to give well. The recipient feels called to make the most of the gift.

Generosity beckons us not only to act generously, but to become connoisseurs of generosity. To fully realize our capacity for giving, we need take delight in the generous acts of others, just as we do in performing them ourselves. We need to be on the lookout for generous perceptions, words, and actions, and when they occur, to acknowledge and savor them. This is one of the human missions in the world: to seek out and appreciate the beauty it contains. Because truly generous acts are among the most beautiful of all, it is only fitting that we try to see them for what they are and admire them. In savoring giving, we also encourage others to develop their capacity for generosity. Like gardeners watering plants, we are helping to nurture goodness in the world around us.

To perceive generously is to understand compassionately. Some acts of giving are poorly conceived. In some cases, we might even wonder if the giver meant to give offense. Yet viewing giving generously means looking for the best intentions and doing what we can to make sure that gifts have the best outcome. An act of spontaneous generosity should be the last place we find an occasion for criticism, sarcasm, or resentment. Some adolescents and adults do not have a great deal of experience with giving or may have grown rusty at it. Like anything else, becoming proficient requires practice, and our initial efforts may not realize the success we would hope for. Yet every person's development provides opportunities to nurture the habit of generosity, and we need to be generous ourselves to prevent them from being nipped in the bud.

The fact that there can be no giver without a recipient calls us to cultivate our capacity to receive graciously. How can others learn to give well if we do not receive well? Such grace can be as simple as writing sincere notes of thanks to those who give us a gift. But it extends far beyond that. Gifts are generally less significant than acts of kindness, and kindness is the form of generosity that we most need to attend to and relish. If we are not genuinely gracious, then we are not truly generous. If we let our pride get in the way, obstinately refusing to accept anything from anyone, then we are operating with a false self-image. Our presumption of self-sufficiency prevents us from showing the appropriate appreciation for others' kindnesses. We show how generous we are no less in receiving than in giving.

Every time a spirit of generosity emerges, we are presented with a golden opportunity. It is an opportunity to marvel at a beauty that is far deeper, more enduring, and more humanly fulfilling than a fine face or a comely figure. No less than the starry night sky, a majestic waterfall, or an infant's smile, witnessing generosity is one of the most sublime pleasures we can know. To let such moments pass by unnoticed is to convict ourselves of gross insensibility and ingratitude. Hence each act of generosity is also a learning opportunity. The greater the generosity, the more we can learn from it. For the sake of our development as human beings, we should be on the lookout for the most generous among us, and we should spend time getting to know them. They may not be pundits or professors, but they have a great deal to teach us.

In the wake of a natural disaster, a woman working with a national charitable organization offered a handicrafts class for small children. Her efforts provided child care for parents who needed time to get their lives back together, and it gave the children an opportunity to play at a time when schools were shut down, playmates had been separated, and toys were in scarce supply. On the first day of class, the children immediately immersed themselves in making decorative objects using wooden sticks, glue, glitter, markers, and the like. On the day of their last class, each child had accumulated quite a treasure trove of handicrafts. The teacher asked what they would do with them. Without any hesitation, the children decided to give their creations as gifts to other disaster victims.

Many of these children had lost their houses. Their home lives had been profoundly disrupted. The class enabled them to find joy in making their crafts, and the children took pride in hearing their work praised by others. Yet instead of keeping them for themselves, their first impulse was to give them away. They wanted to lift others' spirits using the best resource they had, perhaps the best crafts many of them had ever made. Technically speaking, their work was far from perfect. Professional artisans could have done much better. Yet the children had done their best, and they were brimming with excitement about at the prospect of sharing their work with others. The thought of brightening someone else's life filled them with joy.

16

WHO IS EXPENDABLE?

In his 2000 book, *Black Hawk Down: A Story of Modern War,* Mark Bowden offers a riveting account of a U.S. combat operation that took place in the nation of Somalia in 1993. The operation was intended to capture the lieutenants of a Somali warlord, but it went disastrously awry when U.S. helicopters were downed by rocket fire. Eventually, one hundred U.S. servicemen were left stranded in the well-armed, hostile city of Mogadishu. During the ensuing chaotic battles in the streets, eighteen U.S. servicemen lost their lives, and many more were injured. The number of Somali casualties may be conservatively estimated in the hundreds.

Press accounts of the conflict emphasized the U.S. soldiers' reluctance to leave behind their comrades, including even the bodies of those killed in combat. This sentiment was highlighted in director Ridley Scott's 2001 film *Blackhawk Down*, which was marketed with the slogan, "Leave No Man Behind." It is true that a task force of ninety-nine men did remain overnight in extremely hostile territory to avoid abandoning a comrade's body. In subsequent interviews, however, several commanders admitted to Bowden that had the opportunity presented itself, they would have left dead soldiers behind to evacuate their beleaguered troops.

Why would soldiers remain true to the motto "leave no man behind" even if it meant placing themselves in harm's way and perhaps even jeopardizing the success of a mission? In Mogadishu, part of the answer lay in recent events. Reports in the world press had featured disturbing photos of the bodies of fallen U.S. soldiers being disfigured by Somali mobs.

Many of the Army Ranger troops on the ground in Mogadishu reported that they felt drawn toward their comrades' helicopter crash

sites to prevent the desecration of their bodies. Prior to the operation, the men had agreed that no such dishonor would ever befall
their comrades. They were motivated in part by pride in their uni-
form, a determination never to allow their service and their nation
to be subjected to such humiliation. Running still deeper, however,
was their sense of loyalty to one another. Many felt they could never
live with themselves if they abandoned a comrade, either in life or
in death. Said one, "You just don't let that happen to a brother in
arms."

Whether formal or informal, a code that prohibits soldiers from
abandoning a comrade promotes an extraordinary sense of solidarity.
If we are so devoted to our comrades that we would sacrifice our
lives rather than allow a fellow soldier's body to be captured or dese-
crated by hostile forces, then we will naturally exhibit great cohesion
as a fighting unit. When the situation appears grim, we will be better
equipped to subordinate our own fears to our shared mission. Each
of us would risk our lives for the soldiers in our unit, and we know
they would do the same for us.

To label any member of a unit expendable would undermine this
sense of solidarity. It would suggest that some lives are not worth the
sacrifice. At a particular moment of battle, abandoning a comrade
may seem the most prudent course of action. Perhaps so doing would
keep two lives, a dozen lives, or even hundreds of lives out of harm's
way. But once such a decision is taken, things will never be the same.
The sense of mutual commitment will be deeply wounded.

When we say that someone is expendable, we supplant collective
loyalty with individualism. Each of us is prepared to defend the others only so long as the level of danger remains low. When we determine that a comrade is not worth fighting for, we declare that other
things are more important to us. Should we march ahead into danger
or bail out and flee to safety? So-called acts of cowardice threaten
a military unit partly through a breakdown in discipline. But the
breakdown in solidarity is even more damaging.

A similar theme runs through another war film, director Steven
Spielberg's *Saving Private Ryan*. During World War II, a mother receives three separate notifications that one of her sons has died in
combat. When army commanders realize that her fourth son, Pri-

vate Ryan, is stationed behind enemy lines, they deploy a team to find him and bring him safely home. Along the way, the soldiers tasked with saving Private Ryan confront numerous trials and suffer many losses. Yet they carry on. To them, such sacrifices are warranted by their compassion for a family they have never met.

These portrayals of loyalty among soldiers provide insights into what it means to be bound together in community. They especially shed light on the notion of expendability, and they highlight a choice that is always before us. We can say that everyone is expendable. Or we can say that no one is expendable. We may think that in between we see intermediate possibilities. Perhaps some people are expendable and others are not. In fact, however, such intermediate alternatives are deeply problematic. As soon as we say that any one of us is expendable, we say in principle that everyone is. Why?

How do we determine expendability? Is it a lack of wealth, honor, or good works? Is it soundness of body or mind? Tomorrow each of us could suffer a financial catastrophe, a sudden loss of reputation, or a moral failure. We might also suffer a medical catastrophe that leaves us physically or mentally disabled. According to the Bible, such misfortunes befell even Job, the greatest man in the all the East, upright and righteous before God. If they could happen to Job, they could certainly happen to us. If expendability is an option, then an accident of fate might render any one of us expendable.

We can become progressively richer, stronger, and more famous, but we cannot completely insulate ourselves against disaster. To suppose that we could ever achieve a state of invincibility would be supreme self-deception. Nor would a state of invincibility be good for us, morally speaking. Events that compromise our wealth, fame, power, and comfort do not always work to our detriment. Adversity does not invariably destroy character. In some cases, it builds it. In suffering, we sometimes deepen our capacity to respond compassionately to the afflictions of others. The awareness of both our liability to suffering and the fragility of our flourishing makes us full members of the human community.

Consider the very weakest among us, those least able to fend for themselves, defend themselves, and contribute to the lives of others. Specifically, consider the severely mentally and physically handicapped, human beings whose capabilities are sometimes so limited that they are incapacitated. Some remain confined to a bed, even dependent on life-support apparatus, all their lives. How should we treat them? How much are their lives worth? Do their failure to contribute to the community and the high costs associated with their care render them expendable, people without whom the human community would be better off?

Such questions are not merely hypothetical. During Germany's Third Reich, the Nazis instituted a "mercy killing" program they labeled T4, after the address of the government office in Berlin from which it was administered. It was created for two reasons. First, the nation faced an economic crisis, and resources were scarce. Second, its founders aimed to protect the biological purity of the German people by eliminating individuals they regarded as "worthless eaters." The initial targets were children suffering from disabilities, deformities, and mental illnesses. Such children were removed from their families and placed in special "hospitals." There they were put to death by gas, suffocation, injection, poisoning, or starvation. Eventually, approximately 240,000 human beings were "euthanized."

The Nazi T4 program dramatizes the profound danger of labeling any person or group of people expendable. First we learn to regard some people as unnecessary. Then difficult circumstances transform expendability into a threat. The prerogative of withholding or withdrawing assistance may mutate into an irresistible duty to cast out, or even to kill. We can quickly forget that compassion represents one of the essential human excellences.

The Nazi example reminds us that moral progress is not synonymous with a stated intention to do good. In some cases, our efforts to make things better may actually make them worse. If our programs to promote health and conquer disease render us less tolerant of the afflictions of others, then they harm all of us. Imbedded in every impulse toward perfection are the seeds of intolerance and even bigotry. In attempting to perfect our bodies we must take care lest we corrupt our souls.

Acknowledging the dangers of labeling some among us expendable does not imply that we must completely overlook our differences. Chance, fate, or divine providence has placed us in different life stations. Most of us were born whole of mind and body, and a smaller number possess special abilities that most of us lack. Others have been burdened with disabilities. In both cases, some of us have made more of our natural endowment than others. Some have done little with what we were given, and others have managed to do a great deal. We can admit that fate plays an important role in determining our life prospects without granting that it also determines our human worth.

Human worth is not correlated with our abilities and level of achievement. Everyone is endowed with the same human dignity, regardless of what language we speak, the thickness of our wallets, or the length of our resumes. This realization is one of the core geniuses of the United States of America, the longest-lived republic in human history. Its founders recognized the existence of universal human rights that do not depend on wealth, honor, or good works. No citizen's vote counts for more than another's. Every person counts just the same.

When we begin to separate ourselves into "us" and "them," we inevitably begin questioning the worth of others. We begin to suppose that we represent the model of humanity, and that those who do not conform to our image are somehow less than human, or at least less human than we. They may suffer, but they cannot suffer the way we do, because they cannot walk or talk, or they do not have a job, or they have not read the books we have read. And because they do not suffer the way we suffer, their pain is somehow less significant and more easily overlooked. When it comes to allocating even such basic resources as education and healthcare, those who are different from us begin to seem expendable.

In fact, disability of one sort or another is a universal human experience. Some of us cannot talk, others cannot hear, others cannot see, and still others cannot speak. Some of us cannot walk, others cannot write, and others cannot feed ourselves. Even those of us who are completely able-bodied, however, have known disability. Some of us are not very good at math, others are clumsy, others are tone deaf, and still others are terrified of speaking in public. Some of us

are afraid of spiders, others of crowds, and still others of police officers. Try as we might, most of us could never be world-class pianists,
professional basketball players, or chess grand masters.

Viewed through this lens, disability is more the rule than the ex-
ception. It is not a special curse, but a form of human variation.
People with disabilities face special challenges, but sometimes they
are able to turn those challenges into opportunities. Their disabilities
create special challenges for us, but if we try, we can often turn those
challenges into opportunities for ourselves as well. For example, who
says that dependence is a bad thing? Far from limiting or disgracing
us, it is our interdependence that sets us free and distinguishes us as
human beings and communities. Perhaps collaboration, not isolation, is the key to our liberation.

We mistakenly suppose that the differences between us weaken us.
We think that uniformity and homogeneity are the keys to a harmo-
nious and successful community. But in fact, the differences between
us are frequently our greatest sources of strength. Diversity shows us
that things can be different. It fosters our ability to adapt and innovate. It enhances our resourcefulness. Disabilities help us see more
clearly what really makes us human, and they help us care for one another more humanely by showing us what we really need from one
another. When we look carefully, we realize that disability resides as
much in us as in the disabled person, and we discover abilities to care
we never knew we had.

Likewise, it is a mistake to suppose that our greatness lies solely in
our differences. We are physically fit, or well-educated, or successful,
and that sets us apart from other people. It is our differences, we suppose, that makes us great. In fact, however, it is not our differences
that make us great, but our commonalities. We become great human
beings not because we see the differences between us, but because
we see the common experiences and purposes that bind us together.
Great figures of the twentieth century such as Winston Churchill,
Martin Luther King, Jr., and Mother Teresa became great precisely
because they realized that we are all in this together.

This is the genius of the military perspective. Through shared effort and hardship, every soldier in the unit learns to regard each comrade as a brother, someone for whom it is right to risk even life itself.

The question is whether we can develop and sustain a similar level of loyalty to one another in peacetime, when we are not united by a common enemy bent on our destruction. If we attain greatness, it will not be because we have learned to distinguish between who is expendable and who is indispensable, but because we have learned to see that we are all in this together, and that even the weakest among us are no less worthy as human beings than anyone else.

17

HOW MUCH AND HOW WELL?

One of the best-known stories about giving in the New Testament concerns the poor widow and her two coins (Luke 21:1–4). Jesus was teaching in the temple. He saw crowds of people walking by, dropping their offerings into the collection box. Then he saw a poor widow put in two pennies. He said, "The plain truth is that this widow has given by far the largest offering today. All these others made offerings that they'll never miss; she gave extravagantly what she couldn't afford—she gave her all!" This story is usually regarded as a beautiful tale of sacrifice and devotion, but it is also puzzling. The widow clearly needed every meager cent merely to survive. What sense could it make to praise people for giving away their livelihood? Is the widow not committing suicide by giving away all that she had? What kind of example is this to set for the poor?

The story can be interpreted in many ways. One possibility is that Jesus is speaking of the widow not in laudatory terms, but as a cautionary tale. No one should give to the point that they exhaust all their resources, leaving themselves with nothing, for in so doing they jeopardize their own survival. Another would be that the amount we give is less important than the spirit in which it is given. What matters is not what she gives but why and how she gives it. Another would be the interpretation that the absolute quantity of a gift is less important than its relative value to the giver. Ten cents from a person who has only a dollar is just as laudable as a million-dollar gift from someone who has ten million dollars. Still another interpretation would be that we should be prepared to give everything we have.

It is disturbing to contemplate the possibility that Jesus is warning his hearers not to behave like the widow. And yet such an interpretation follows naturally if we focus strictly on the practical impact of the gift. Perhaps we are meant to see the widow as a fool, duped by religious authorities into believing that "every gift counts," and blind to the fact that her gift is of no consequence. In relation to the size of others' offerings, the widow's contribution does not even amount to two drops in a large bucket. It is worth nothing, a waste, an absurdity. Yet if this is true, why would Jesus stress that it is the largest offering of the day? It could be that he is speaking ironically. But then why would he stress that the others will never miss their gifts? Surely it is to emphasize that even though her gift is small in absolute terms, she will miss it dearly, and it is precisely on those grounds that it is the largest of the day.

It is difficult to sustain the interpretation that the spirit of giving is paramount. Though many have attempted to extract such a meaning from the story, the text itself provides no information on why the widow gives. For all we know, she could be giving out of a sense of guilt. Perhaps she has even improperly taken money from the collection box on prior occasions. The only thing we can confidently infer about her motive is its strength. She feels so strongly called to give that she is prepared to part with everything she has. Her gift is an act of extravagance, of magnanimity. Even though she has very little to give, she is able to give in abundance, with a greater degree of generosity than even the rich people.

This leads naturally to the interpretation that gifts must be appraised in part by the sacrifice they represent to those who give them. The richest person is not necessarily the best equipped to be generous, and just because a person's monetary gift is the largest in absolute terms does not mean it is the most praiseworthy. We cannot simply divide donors into gold, silver, and bronze categories based on the size of the checks they write and assume we are appropriately representing the relative merits of their gifts. Along these lines, it is important that she is not only a woman but a widow, someone in biblical times without any means of support. She probably did not know where her next two cents were coming from. It is also important that she put not one but two pennies in the collection box. By contributing two, she proves that she has more than one. She is not offering the smallest possible gift, which makes it even more likely that she is giving everything she has.

The most fitting interpretation, then, is that she is giving all she has, a reading that is supported by Jesus' own explanation. She literally gave her all. Why would it be important that she gave everything she had? In what sense might we regard such a gift as morally or spiritually exemplary, given its adverse impact on her own prospects for survival? Perhaps it is only when we give our all, or at least only when we are prepared to give our all, that we truly understand the appropriate place of wealth and property in the economy of human goods. Most rich people would have regarded the prospect of possessing only two pennies as unthinkable. How could anyone get through the day, even live for a single minute, with only two pennies to their name? And yet the widow is not only able to get through the day, she is even prepared to give what little she has, for God's sake.

This parable alludes to a potential tyranny behind our impulse to measure gifts. The tyranny is that we soon find ourselves so fixated on measuring and ranking gifts according to some objective standard that we forget the larger context and deeper meaning that inspire giving. Simply put, all important results cannot be quantified. When we forget this, we frequently end up distorting more than clarifying the true meaning of a gift. What is measurable? The dollar value of goods and services. If we try to assign a dollar value to every gift, soon we may view all instances of generosity strictly in terms of their lowest common denominator. Soon the means for measuring the goal—that is, dollar value—becomes a proxy for the goal itself. Generosity becomes a matter of money, the number of dollars that have changed hands.

Consider another arena where the tyranny of measurement is very much in evidence. In public education, we are placing increasing emphasis on measuring educational outcomes, such as graduation rates and test scores. Such measures direct the flow of dollars among teachers and schools to a greater extent than ever before. Yet what do the tests test? They focus on educational outcomes that are easy to measure, such as vocabulary and basic math skills. As for the curriculum, more complex subjects not represented on the tests tend to fall by the wayside. The cultural side of education, including such subjects as physical education, art, and music, suffer funding cuts or get dropped entirely. Our vision of an educated person becomes narrower and more superficial, and education itself becomes a testocracy. How quickly we forget that we no more educate students by testing them than we fatten cattle by weighing them.

What is the bottom line of a philanthropic organization? Is it the amount of money it raises in a fiscal year? Is it the funds it disburses in grants? Is it the value of its investment portfolio? If we look seriously at the outcomes of the outcomes assessment movement in education, we might be inclined to think twice before supposing that the output of philanthropic organizations can be rendered in strictly economic terms. Perhaps we simply cannot assess generosity or philanthropic excellence in monetary terms. Perhaps generosity is not just about writing checks, and philanthropy is not just about fundraising and grant making. Albert Einstein famously said that not everything that counts can be counted, and not every thing that can be counted counts. In terms of philanthropy, what counts, and to what degree should we be trying to count it?

It is quite possible that the values of philanthropy are not the same as the values of business. In business, we might assume that the richest people are the most successful, the ones who have created the most value for others. In philanthropy, however, the richest people are not necessarily the most successful. For one thing, there is no guarantee that a rich person will be moved to give. More importantly, it is simply unnecessary to be rich to be an exemplar of generosity. The mere fact that a group of potential donors has the most money does not prove that they will or even can be the best philanthropists. To say otherwise would be like assuming that the largest people make the best athletes. Athletic excellence is not strictly correlated with size, and philanthropic excellence is not tightly correlated with wealth.

Many people want philanthropy to be more businesslike. They believe that philanthropic organizations need to do a better job of defining and assessing outcomes, holding themselves accountable for results, and reducing inefficiency in their operations. How do philanthropic organizations know if they are doing a good job? How do they know if they are performing poorly? How could they know? Should they evaluate themselves in terms of the intent of their founder, their charter, their mission statement, the morale of their board members or employees, the welfare of those to whom they give, the state of their communities, the assessments of peer organizations, or their public approval rating?

Merely giving away money is not good enough. If it were, it would be simple to appraise philanthropists and philanthropic organizations in terms of their annual outlays. But philanthropic excellence calls for more. Wasting money is not acceptable. Every philanthropic organization wants to serve as a good steward of the resources that have been placed in its charge. Yet efficiency is not enough either, because it does not address why we give. We are moved to give not by a desire to ensure that nothing is wasted, but from an inspiration to help. Mere efficiency is less important than building a sense of philanthropic efficacy, at both the individual and community levels. We want to feel called upon to give, but we also need to know that our giving can and will make a difference.

This is an important drawback of the bureaucratization and professionalization of philanthropy. Ultimately, we want people to be committed to service not because it is how they collect their paycheck, but because they believe it is the best life for them to lead. The more philanthropy becomes professionalized, the less ordinary people may feel they have something to contribute. Those on the outside of philanthropic organizations may ask, "How can we, with our meager resources and lack of training, ever compete with the professionals? Perhaps we should leave the giving to them." Yet philanthropic amateurism is vital. It not only does more to promote the flourishing of the giver. It also tends to achieve a better fit between the hopes of particular givers and the needs of particular recipients. Moreover, it may foster a greater degree of innovation in giving.

We cannot afford to make ordinary people feel philanthropically incompetent or irrelevant. Yet that is precisely where the professionalization of philanthropy often leads. At its extreme, it leaves people feeling that they have nothing to contribute. When a natural disaster strikes, we feel incapable of more than worrying while we wait for the disaster relief agencies to show up. Taken to the extreme, the professionalization of philanthropy promotes what psychologists call learned helplessness. We see poverty, or disease, or suffering, and we feel that there is nothing we can do. Instead of learned helplessness, philanthropic organizations should foster a sense of learned helpfulness. A strong philanthropic sector should promote, not undermine, our sense of philanthropic efficacy. It is important that we use funds efficiently, but it is even more important that we cultivate the habit of generosity.

Consider the role of so-called "microfinance" and "microenterprise" in the developing world. The goal of such initiatives is to extend small loans to the extremely poor so they can purchase capital. A Bangladeshi organization offers such services with a view to cultivating social connections. It makes loans to groups of four to five women to help them start small businesses selling produce and crafts in marketplaces. The amounts of money involved are very small, yet the returns on investment can be very large. Over time, these groups of women become less dependent on outside aid, not more dependent. If a member of the group suffers a loss, the other members come to her aid. No formal reporting mechanisms are required, for such information travels by word of mouth, as in a family. Their sense of philanthropic efficacy is not undermined, but enhanced.

All gifts are important, not just the ones with the most zeroes. Even small gifts may produce huge returns if the resources are invested wisely. When we talk about assessing the return on investment, money is the easiest thing to measure. But there are other kinds of gifts and other kinds of returns. Time, effort, and commitment are at least as important as money. A person may write a check in a minute, but the effect of that act may be much less significant than face-to-face interaction over hours with people in need. Writing a check often serves to end a conversation, punctuating the response to an appeal for aid, while rolling up our shirtsleeves means things are just getting started. When we get involved, our understanding of others' needs is deepened in ways that merely handing over money can never provide.

There are different kinds of poverty. There is the kind of poverty we all know, financial poverty. But there is also poverty of the imagination. We can be poor not only in terms of material wealth but morally and spiritually as well. Philanthropic organizations need to ask themselves this question: What are we doing to engage and nourish the philanthropic imaginations of those whose contributions we solicit, not to mention the members of our own staff? And what are we doing to inspire the imaginations of our recipients? Are we helping them become the generous human beings they are meant to be? Are we fostering forms of generosity that extend beyond money? Are we cultivating compassion and nurturing human understanding?

How do we know what others need and what we are capable of contributing to them? How do we know what we need and what others are capable of contributing to us? To answer these questions, we must know others and we must know ourselves. To excel at generosity, in other words, we must be knowers. We need to know the needs and opportunities available to us, our disposition to give, the means at our disposal, and the larger ends that shape our giving. In this sense, philanthropy is inextricably bound up with philosophy, for in both cases the search for truth lies at the core. Because an incurious philanthropy is necessarily an ineffective philanthropy, philanthropy depends on curiosity. We cannot satisfy our curiosity unless we inquire, and we cannot get answers to our inquiries unless we listen. So to excel philanthropically, we must excel at listening.

Consider the philanthropic mission of colleges and universities. To some degree, they are about transmitting specialized knowledge and technical skills. Yet mere transmission is only part of their mission. At their best, they have another aim, which is to prepare human beings to lead fulfilling lives. To do so, they need to engage students in a form of discourse that is less dogmatic than exploratory. Where the most important knowledge is concerned, students need to pose the questions for themselves, and pursue their own answers. We cannot, strictly speaking, measure the results of this inquiry. Yet it is nonetheless subject to critique, testable in some way. In carrying out such a critique, everything is not up for grabs. For example, we proceed with the commitment that knowledge is fundamentally preferable to ignorance.

What do we need to know? Some might argue that we most need to know the current circumstances of the people in the world around us. To be philanthropically informed, we need to be voracious consumers of news, closely attuned to the latest events of the day. After all, if we do not monitor newspapers, television, and the Internet to stay abreast of current events, how can we be prepared to respond to the latest human calamity, whether it be acts of warfare or terrorism, natural disasters, outbreak of diseases, or economic catastrophes? Yet saying that we must know what is happening does not establish the news of the day as the most important focus of inquiry. An educated philanthropist may rely at least as much on other sources.

Suppose, for example, that the only source of knowledge available to a group of philanthropists is television news. Let it be a room full of televisions, each tuned to a different news channel. How much insight would such people enjoy? Although they would know instantly about every newsworthy human calamity, their breadth and depth of understanding might prove deficient. In addition to knowing what is happening today, philanthropists need to understand the broad sweep of human history. How much insight into human suffering and flourishing would news media offer? Would they require supplementation by poems, epics, novels, or the great works of philosophy and religion? A liberal education is at least as important a philanthropic resource as ready access to breaking news.

It is not enough that we give, even if we give in great quantities. More important than whether we give or even how much we give is why we give. It is not only important. It is all-important. In the balance of why, everything hangs. In responding to it we reveal our understanding of the goodness of giving. Going to college can be a means to earning a better living. Studying philanthropy can be a means to raising and giving away more money. Yet there is more to going to college than learning a trade, and more to philanthropy than moving money. At its best, college provides insights whose enduring value is largely immeasurable, and the same can be said for philanthropy. In deepening our understanding of the human situation, we open up new opportunities to share, and in sharing more completely we gain deeper understanding. Even though such sharing and understanding resist measurement, they are among the most real and vital aspects of our lives.

18

ARE WE HOSPITABLE?

Numerous terms of derision might have been applied—unkempt, grungy, disheveled. The family came from an economically depressed region in the southern part of the state. The parents were unemployed, and neither they nor their child looked as though they had changed clothes or bathed in a week. It was not just that they were unkempt—they were genuinely dirty. Both parents had bad teeth, and their little daughter's tangled hair hung limp and stringy over her dirt-smudged forehead. I walked into the examination room and introduced myself, shook the parents' rough hands, lightly touched the little girl's shoulder, and then stepped over to the sink to wash my hands.

The girl, three years old, had recently suffered several urinary tract infections, and a local physician had referred her to our hospital for further diagnostic testing. My colleagues and I had been asked to perform a test called a voiding cystourethrogram. This would involve placing a catheter into the child's urinary bladder, infusing liquid radiographic contrast material, then using x-rays to see if there was abnormal reversed flow of urine from her bladder up into her kidneys. When present, this condition enables any minor bladder infection to cause a more serious kidney infection. A severe kidney infection could, in turn, cause high blood pressure or even kidney failure later in life.

We placed the little girl on the examination table. Her pale legs looked as though she must have recently played in the dirt. As soon as we inserted the catheter, cloudy, foul-smelling urine began to drain out, indicating that she was currently suffering from an infection. As the contrast filled her bladder, it soon refluxed up into both kidneys. This meant she would need to start taking a small dose of antibiotic each day to protect her kidneys from damage by another infection. Would the family be able to comply with these instructions? I learned that they had no fixed address and were living in temporary public housing. They had no phone number. How different their life must be from mine!

As the bedraggled family left our examination room to go to the urology clinic, a concern descended over me. What would happen to these people—not just in the months and years to come, but today, right here in our hospital? How would they be treated by other families in the waiting room? We care not only for the poor, but also for many privileged families, people with addresses in the very best parts of town. What would they make of these ragamuffins? Would children from the richer side of the tracks avoid playing with the little girl? If these poor people took a seat next to another family, would the others get up and move? Might contact with these people lead some of our more privileged families to resolve not to return to our facility?

What of my colleagues and I? How had we treated this family? Did the receptionist speak with them courteously? How did the patient registrars react to their lack of insurance, their inability to provide even a phone number? Had we spoken to them in loud, slow voices, as we often speak to people we assume to be of subnormal intelligence? Were we offering up cues, some subtle and some not so subtle, that we did not approve of them, perhaps even that we did not want them here?

I found myself musing on the hospitality of our hospital. Hospitality, giving, and generosity are intimately related. Hospitality represents one of our most basic opportunities to care for one another. How do we treat strangers on our own turf, whether that turf happens to be our home, workplace, school, house of worship, community, or nation? Do we ignore strangers? Do we treat them antagonistically? Or do we go out of our way to acknowledge their presence, greet them, and make them feel welcome? Are we resentful and stingy toward visitors, or do we treat them with a full and generous heart? Of all the workplace settings in which hospitality might manifest itself, surely it is in the hospital that this excellence would shine.

Yet, pondering the hospitality of our hospital, I was not so sure.

There are many forces in contemporary healthcare that tend to make physicians and patients strangers to one another. Physicians believe we are under pressing time constraints that require us to limit the amount of time we spend with any particular patient. If we take too long, decreasing the number of patients we can see or making patients wait a long time, patient satisfaction scores may suffer, and revenue targets may not be met. Moreover, our population is more mobile, and relocating typically requires finding a new doctor. In other cases, even though we stay put, changes in employment or health insurance necessitate changing physicians. Each time such a change takes place, physician and patient meet one another as strangers.

Another factor is our increasingly specialized approach to healthcare. A family physician may care for routine needs, but in the case of serious illness requiring hospitalization, we are likely to find ourselves under the care of a battery of specialists. This might include a cardiologist, pulmonologist, gastroenterologist, neurologist, general surgeon, and so on. And physicians alone are not the whole story. The healthcare team includes numerous additional members: nurses, technologists, physical and respiratory therapists, social workers, dieticians, housekeepers, and food service workers, among many others. Again, such people are often strangers to the patient.

Another factor is the increasing technological sophistication of medicine. In bygone eras, when the physician's diagnostic and therapeutic armamentarium was considerably simpler, a compassionate "bedside manner" represented one of the principal services physicians could offer patients. Today, however, the science and technology of medicine are so complex that health professionals often become engrossed in this side of our practice. We are so busy pondering what test to order and what therapy to prescribe that we forget how intimidating a place the hospital can seem to patients and families.

Part of the problem with hospitality is that no single healthcare profession claims such a basic excellence as its mission. Busy nurses may think it is the receptionists' role to make patients feel welcome, and busy physicians may regard it as the nurses' responsibility. Each of us protests, "But hospitality is not in my job description." But in fact, hospitality is everyone's responsibility. Every person who works in the hospital, from the chief executive officer and the president of the medical staff to the people who serve food and mop the floors, enjoys regular opportunities to extend the hand of hospitality. Even discount retailers sometimes do a better job recognizing this opportunity than hospitals. Many station a greeter at the store entrance, whose role is to extend a greeting and answer patrons' questions. Some even refer to customers as "guests," thereby promoting an attitude of hospitality in the minds of their employees.

In some respects, hospitality is a relatively new problem in medicine's history. The Hippocratic Oath reads, "Whatever houses I may visit, I will enter for the benefit of the sick. . . ." It assumes that physicians make house calls, going to patients rather than expecting patients to come to physicians. In the Hippocratic model of healthcare, the physician is the guest, and the responsibility for hospitality rests with the family whose home the physician enters. In our contemporary model, however, patients come to physicians. Especially the very sickest and most vulnerable patients must be cared for in the physician's domain, the hospital. As a result, the patient becomes the guest. The responsibilities of host devolve to the physician and other health professionals.

How much time in our health professions curricula do we devote to hospitality? In my own medical training, virtually none. We are so busy teaching future physicians anatomy, physiology, pathology, diagnostics, therapeutics, and a host of other scientific and clinical disciplines that no time is left for simple graciousness. Time is even tighter in residency, where the clinical demands often seem overwhelming. A topic such as hospitality probably strikes some medical educators as too soft. They might argue that students should have learned how to play the role of host long before they matriculated in medical school. They should have learned it as children at home, or in scouting or Sunday school.

But what if some did not get it there? And what if hospitality, like other moral virtues, needs to be nourished by frequent example and encouragement? How many medical educators ensure that physicians in training have opportunities to see and emulate great hosts in action? When it comes to shining as a doctor or a nurse, mastering the science and technology is not sufficient. To excel at what we do, we must be able to put ourselves in the patient's place, to see the complexities of healthcare from a stranger's point of view, and to appreciate what we would need if we were the ones looking up from the hospital bed.

The very term "hospital" tells us something important. It comes from the same Latin root as our word hospitality, *hospitalis,* which means "of a guest." This in turn is derived from *hostis,* a root meaning "stranger." Hospitals were once places of shelter and rest for travelers who, throughout most of human history, could not simply check into a hotel. Later, the hospital became a charitable institution that cared for the aged, infirm, and orphaned. Only relatively recently, during the twentieth century, did the term acquire the connotation of a high-tech institution where the ill and injured receive sophisticated medical care from an array of healthcare specialists.

The names of many hospitals reveal the hospitable intentions of their founders. For example, many boast names such as Home Hospital, Community Hospital, and Family Hospital. Others take their names from religious traditions, such as Methodist Hospital, Presbyterian Hospital, Lutheran Hospital, Good Samaritan Hospital, and Jewish Hospital. Particularly in the Roman Catholic tradition, hospitals are often named after saints, such as St. Francis and St. Vincent. In each case, such names reveal the fundamentally philanthropic impulse that spawned the institution. They were founded not to optimize patient throughput, healthcare revenue, or corporate operating margins, but to care for needy and suffering human beings.

Ironically, during the twentieth century, the term "hospital" became associated with a disease. Called hospitalism, it reached epidemic proportions in some nations during and after the great European wars, when many newly orphaned infants were placed in institutions. Even though these infants were regularly bathed and fed, they often manifested severe growth retardation, and some died. Initially, investigators suspected they were being exposed to some unknown infectious agent or toxin. Over time they realized that the real culprit was a deficiency of human interaction, and especially a lack of touch. Today hospitalism is called failure to thrive. We clearly recognize the vital necessity of the human touch in its prevention. To survive, as well as to develop fully, human beings need something akin to tender loving care. In pediatric care we have managed to put these lessons into practice reasonably well, but this aspect of care is still lacking for many elderly and disabled patients.

In the hospice movement of the late twentieth century, we see an effort to return to the hospital's roots in caring for the suffering. As medicine developed more effective therapies for diseases, we became increasingly focused on curing patients. While this shift in orientation worked well for those with curable disorders, it created problems for patients whose conditions were incurable, such as advanced cancer. We tended to ignore such patients, mistakenly assuming that we could do nothing for them. Reacting to patients' sense of abandonment, hospice programs have created models for care of those we no longer hope to cure. They provide comfort and companionship to the terminally ill and dying. Even where restoring health and vanquishing pain are no longer possible, we can still care compassionately for the suffering.

Though the hospital as we know it is a relatively recent invention, hospitality is as old as mankind. In ancient times, travelers depended on the hospitality of indigenous peoples for their very survival. In the arid lands of the Bible, water was absolutely essential, and towns and settlements were generally built around water sources. Travelers who could not gain access to water were doomed. Moreover, food was scarce in the desert, and travelers could not sustain themselves by living off the land. Nature alone, in other words, was not sufficiently hospitable. Travelers depended on the kindness of strangers.

Of course, hospitality has never been a risk-free endeavor. Strangers are, by definition, unknown, and it is impossible to discern their intentions with certainty. Is it prudent to trust them? There is an ever-present danger that a guest will turn out to be a thief, a rapist, or an assassin. Consider the fate of Homer's King Menelaus, who graciously opened up his home to a royal visitor from Troy, only to find that Prince Paris stole his beautiful wife, Helen. The consequence of this offense against hospitality was nothing less than the decade-long Trojan War.

Consider the fate of the Trojans themselves. They were too quick to believe that the Greeks had abandoned the siege of their city, eagerly accepting their parting gift. The Trojan horse was hollow, however, and under cover of night the Greek warriors hidden within emerged, threw open the city's gates to their waiting comrades, and sacked Troy. Hosts do not diminish only their material resources by tending to strangers. They also place themselves at risk. To appreciate some of this hazard in our own day, we need only imagine ourselves behind the wheel of a car debating whether to pull over to the side of the road to give a stranger a lift.

There are also moral and cultural hazards in contact with foreigners. What if their ways are not like ours? What if, in the words of the first great anthropologist, Herodotus, they do not say what we say about the gods? How might an exotic visitor affect the minds and hearts of our young people? Might they be lured away to other lands, other cultures, other religions?

Preserving moral, cultural, and especially religious purity was of paramount concern to ancient sects such as the Pharisees, Sadducees, and Essenes, who therefore separated themselves from others, seeking to remain pure by remaining apart. Their communities were closed to strangers, and they rejected everyone who was not part of their group. In the famous Bible parable of the Good Samaritan, the priest and the Levite walk right past the wounded man, perhaps in order to avoid contamination, while only the Samaritan, the man with no purity to protect, stops and renders aid.

Against the temptation to withhold hospitality and think only of ourselves, the ancient poets offer poignant reminders of how things ought to be done. In the Abrahamic and Homeric traditions, the importance of kindness to strangers is stressed again and again. In fact, the very genealogy of the Abrahamic tradition is rooted in hospitality. Consider, for example, the events in chapter 18 of Genesis. Abraham sees three strangers approaching his tent in the distance. Does he retreat in fear, sealing off his household from all contact with them?

No, quite the reverse, he immediately runs out to meet them, bows low to the ground, calls for water to wash their feet, provides shelter, and offers them food. He provides no mere morsels of bread, but prepares a feast of fine cakes, milk and butter, and even the meat of his finest calf. Abraham shows himself to be righteous and worthy through his conduct as a host. His reward is nothing short of miraculous. He and his aged wife Sarah, long past the age of childbearing, are told by their divine visitors that they will have a son, Isaac. From this son shall arise a great and mighty nation. In this story, hospitality proves to be not merely restorative for the stranger, but also generative for the host.

An even more remarkable example of hospitality occurs in the very next chapter. Lot, living in Sodom, is visited by two angels. He, too, bows low to the ground, offers them lodging, and prepares a great feast for them. During the evening, the men of Sodom surround the house and demand that the strangers be brought forth so that they may know them. Lot pleads with them to refrain from this wickedness, and, in an effort to protect the guests to whom he has extended his protection, offers the crowd his two virgin daughters instead.

Great in number, the gathered men of Sodom do not see themselves as vulnerable in the same way as the strangers. Thus they do not feel obliged to extend kindness. They see the strangers as mere bodies, useful for their own gratification. Their designs reveal their inmost nature, their readiness to exploit those under their care. Lot, by contrast, will spare himself no sacrifice to live up to his responsibilities as a host. Soon God decrees the destruction of the whole city, but not before Lot and his family heed an angel's warning to flee to safety.

Hospitality is evidently very important to the God of the Hebrew scriptures. It is through their hospitable conduct toward strangers that Abraham and Lot prove themselves worthy of divine favor. The men of Sodom, by contrast, prove themselves unworthy by their readiness to exploit others. Elsewhere in the Hebrew scriptures, God himself shines as host. After their escape from bondage in Egypt, the Israelites are lost in the desert, without the means to sustain themselves. It is only because God extends a helping hand, providing water, food, and clothing, that they are able to survive. He attends to more than their material needs for survival. Without their overlords looking over their shoulders, the Israelites are no longer sure how to conduct themselves. God recognizes this need for moral guidance, and provides them a law in the form of the Ten Commandments.

The moral? As God extended gracious hospitality to the Israelites in the desert, so the Israelites should extend the hand of welcome to humanity. What does it mean biblically to emulate the divine host? It means welcoming strangers into our homes. But it also means more. It means allowing them to harvest the corners of cultivated fields, clothing the naked, providing food, tending the sick, and even including strangers in religious celebrations. Hospitality is not merely prudent. It is an expression of godliness. We should not extend hospitality out of a sense of duty. Instead we should emulate the graciousness of Abraham, who unknowingly entertained God himself. True hospitality is active, transforming stranger into guest and guest into friend. We should, in every sense, share the very best of what we have.

In the Homeric tradition, perhaps the most famous example of hospitality gone awry is that of Polyphemus, the legendary Cyclops, whose story Odysseus tells in Book IX of the *Odyssey*. Odysseus and his men, struggling for years to get home following the decade-long Trojan War, find themselves foraging on the shore of a strange land. It is the land of the Cyclops, a people who have no shipwrights and therefore cannot travel the oceanic world of the ancient Mediterranean. As a result of their inability to travel, they have become lawless and inhuman, taking no account of others.

Odysseus, not knowing where he is, wishes to determine whether he is in the land of a hospitable and humane race or uncivilized savages. When Odysseus and his hungry men venture forth and meet the Cyclops in his cave, Odysseus asks the giant to show them hospitality, warning him of the wrath of Zeus if he fails to do so. Polyphemus, however, merely scoffs at this admonition, replying that the Cyclops do not fear the gods, for they are stronger than the gods.

Inhospitality, it seems, is rooted in pride. The arrogant are inhospitable precisely because they hold themselves higher than strangers, and thus fail to empathize with them. Yet Polyphemus's crime is much worse. Instead of serving Odysseus and his men dinner, he makes a meal of his guests. In the ultimate offense against the responsibilities of a host, he sees Odysseus and his men not as fellow human beings in need, but as mere meat. Plotting his revenge, Odysseus ironically asks the giant, "How can you expect people to visit you when you treat them like this?"

This distortion of the rules of hospitality undergoes a further inversion. Clever Odysseus transforms his host into the worst kind of guest and repays him in kind. He shares his wine with Polyphemus, and then seizes the opportunity presented by the giant's drunkenness to put out his eye. At this point the travelers' problem ceases to be one of garnering welcome and becomes instead an imperative of escape, for the giant has blocked the exit from the cave with a great boulder. Odysseus ties his surviving men and himself to the giant's sheep, whom he must let out to pasture each morning, and they escape with their lives. The one-eyed giant's offenses against hospitality leave him not only completely blinded but utterly humiliated.

In the *Odyssey,* as in the Bible, hospitality is a divinely sanctioned calling. The Greek term for hospitality, *xenia,* was the purview of Zeus himself. The goddess Athena, disguised as a beggar, visits the suitors who have been besieging the house of Odysseus and his wife Penelope in his absence. How do they respond? It is their inhospitable conduct, which they reprise when Odysseus himself returns home under similar disguise, that seals their bloody fate. Again and again in the *Odyssey,* gods arrive in the guise of people who are naked, thirsty, hungry, and innocently imprisoned, and it is by conduct toward the needy that human righteousness is assayed. Again and again, Odysseus himself is washed up on a foreign shore, with nothing to rely on but the hospitality of the indigenous people.

The Homeric epic is filled with images of hospitality—eating, drinking, warm hearths, and storytelling. When we are in a strange place, hospitality can make up for what the land and its law do not provide. Food, water, and shelter are not always ready at hand. Even if material needs are met, we still crave more, as anyone who has checked into a hotel in a strange city can attest. We crave companionship, someone to talk to, to share stories with. The law of the land may proscribe theft and robbery and other crimes, but it cannot mandate hospitality. For that, we need something else; namely, the virtues of compassion and curiosity. Hospitality is an art, and a divinely inspired one at that. In the words of Aristotle, it completes what nature cannot bring to a finish.

The virtue of hospitality asks us an important question about our own safety and comfort. Which makes us truly safer, shielding ourselves from others or being with and for others? The safety of isolation is a superficial one, for it keeps us strangers apart from one another, leaving open the trapdoor that leads to fear and loathing. Habits of perception that underscore the separation between human beings, dividing us into self and other, us versus them, bring out the worst in us. They dehumanize others and fan the fires of hostility. We can reasonably ask whether it would be prudent to be hospitable, for there is certainly risk involved. Yet we can also ask whether it would be prudent to be inhospitable, for in that case both guest and host are unavoidably devalued.

The Bible stories and Homeric stories remind us that the distinctions between guest and host are porous and transitory. As hosts, we do not know who will turn out to be good company. As travelers, we do not know who will turn out to be good hosts. Yet we do know for certain that at various times we will play the roles of both host and guest. Both hosts and guest have responsibilities, and in both cases, those responsibilities turn on respecting the humanity of the other. In this sense, our goodness as hosts and our goodness as guests are intimately related. It is in recognizing ourselves in guests that we become good hosts, and in recognizing the hosts within us that we acquit ourselves best as guests.

These narratives pose another question. Who knows what rough stranger may turn out to be an angel, or a god? Who knows what barefoot traveler may turn out to be Socrates, or Jesus Christ? These stories point out the possibility that every stranger bears the mark of the divine. They suggest that we should recognize and if necessary seek out this divine imprint in everyone who comes to us in need. If we fail to detect it, perhaps the fault lies less with the stranger than with ourselves. To seek it out is to render ourselves vulnerable, but vulnerability is a necessary feature of trust, and trust is a necessary feature of friendship and community, without which no human life would be complete. It is important to be worthy of trust, but it is no less important to be trusting.

To offer hospitality is to make a kind of promise, a promise to care for and protect another person. It cannot be made, at least not in earnest, with resentful grinding of teeth. Instead, it must be made willingly. In fact, it is a promise that calls for celebration, both in the making and the keeping. If we are to flourish as human beings, we need to make and keep promises to care for one another. It is in promising that we first declare ourselves on behalf of something greater than the convenience of the moment. It is an opportunity to state not only what we are, but what we wish to become, and thereby to draw ourselves toward something better.

Particularly in the United States, a nation made up largely of immigrants, hospitality cannot be a matter of indifference. The health of the United States as a nation lies less with its material wealth or its natural endowments than with its openness to outsiders. It is a nation where people enjoy an unusual degree of freedom to make of their lives what they will. Its genius springs largely from a wellspring of diversity—diversity of race, ethnicity, national origin, language, religion, and so on. Eligibility for citizenship is based not on bloodlines, language, or religion, but on commitment to political principles of equality and liberty. America's creed of hospitality was captured by Emma Lazarus: "Give me your tired, your poor, your huddled masses yearning to breathe free."

Centuries ago, China, once perhaps the most advanced civilization in the world, became ossified when it cut itself off from the outside world and soon ceased to innovate. Ancient Athens, by contrast, was a nation of seafarers, in constant contact with the outside world. It was largely through the agora, the international marketplace, that its extraordinarily rich culture was spawned.

To be hospitable in the highest and best sense is not merely to make people comfortable, but to give them opportunities to shine, to be at their best. Master hosts do not overwhelm people with their own magnificence. Instead, they create opportunities to bring out the best in their guests. This is a foundational principle of democracy, to believe in and seek out what is special in every person. It is through our commitment to this principle that we build truly diverse and vibrant communities.

Even the very least among us have great worth, if only we know how to look. If we can see strangers in these terms, we recognize that even the homeliest usually have something worth sharing; for example, stories about their own lives, or other places and times. If we are genuinely curious and take an interest in others, we almost always learn new and interesting things. We see new possibilities in life, and gain a clearer vision of what we want to live for.

One of the highest expressions of this philanthropic attitude is found in stories about Jesus Christ. The Christian tradition, too, offers deep insight into the nature of hospitality. Consider the people with whom Jesus habitually associated. He actively sought out people others regarded as the dregs of society: tax collectors, sinners, Samaritans, and gentiles. He sought out the blind, the lame, lepers, the poor, the blind, the downtrodden, and the possessed. He showed special concern for the last, the lost, and least, the little ones among us. Moreover, he did not merely keep company with them. He ate with them, going out of his way to share table fellowship with the unclean and unwanted. Why?

Eating together is perhaps the oldest and most frequently shared communal ritual. In biblical and Homeric times, to share food was also to share life. More so in Jesus' day than in our own, to eat with someone was to create or acknowledge an intimate bond, a gesture extended only to those with whom one was prepared to enter into deep fellowship. Yet Jesus repeatedly ate with tax collectors and prostitutes and sinners. In doing so, he was emphasizing the equality of host and guest, the common humanity that spans artificial social boundaries. Jesus showed that he trusted even these people, perhaps them most of all, and that they were deserving of his trust. Instead of fearing them, he loved them. In doing so, he provided the model for what he calls in the Gospel of John his one new commandment: "To love one another as I have loved you."

The purpose of eating is not to keep ourselves apart, but to come together. "A man shows himself holy," Jesus said, "not by what he puts into his mouth, but by what comes out of it." The sharing of the table symbolizes the sharing of life. Jesus was indicating that the poor and downtrodden should not be consumed by their humiliation and guilt. He was restoring their dignity and, in so doing, showing that even the very least among us—even the very sickest, poorest, and most anguished—does not lack for humanity. No one, not even the least among us, lacks the means to be kind.

Ironically, it is often not the least among us, but the greatest among us, who seem most prone to forget this insight. The busiest, the best educated, the most highly remunerated, those with the most titles on their letterheads are the ones who forget the human opportunities before us. We suppose our time too important, our heads filled with too many great ideas, to take the time to stop and help someone find his or her way, or to extend the touch of human kindness to someone in obvious distress. All too often, it is the greatest among us who forget who we really are and what we are really about.

When Rousseau's Emile visits the homes of people of different stations in life, he soon realizes that it is in the company of the poor that he is treated most humanely. When Jane Addams reflects on hospitality, she realizes that it is in the company of the poor, in places like workhouses and saloons, that she witnesses the most genuine examples of kindness. The rich young prince Siddhartha does not embark on the road to enlightenment until he first comes into contact with human suffering, an unpleasant reality whose very existence he had not known before.

Genuine kindness is born not from the pursuit of self-perfection, but through the recognition of the needs of others. To care for another means recognizing what the other person is going through. It is in suffering ourselves that we learn to respond most humanely to the suffering of others. What is it like to be dirty, naked, thirsty, hungry, sick, lost, and shunned? Do we know? Do we feel it in the marrow of our bones? If such conditions are completely foreign to us, we are liable to respond with fear instead of compassion.

Hospitality is not merely a chance to look good. It is a chance to be good. More than that, it is a chance really to be. Descartes was wrong. We *are* not because we think. We *are* because we are responsible to others. In a profound sense, we *are* precisely in and through our responses to others. We become what we are, both individually and as parts of families and communities, through others.

One of the most beautiful scenes in the 1994 film *Forrest Gump* exemplifies hospitality. Forrest is being sent off to school and boards the school bus for the first time. As he walks down the aisle looking for a seat, he is repeatedly rejected. One after another, boys and girls tell him, "This seat is taken." No one wants Forrest as a seatmate. Then Forrest hears "the most beautiful sound I ever heard." A little girl says to him, "You can sit here." A beautiful moment: a frightened human being made to feel welcome through another's simple kindness.

The biblical and Homeric narratives remind us where we are most likely to encounter the divine. It is not in lofty religious poetry, dazzling baroque art, rich hymnal tones, or soaring cathedral spires. Instead it is in the eyes of others, and perhaps mainly there, that we see God. Above all, it is through the ailing, dirty, barefoot, lost, and bedraggled stranger that we are called to be hospitable.

19

RULES AND ASPIRATIONS

Since its founding, the Center on Philanthropy at Indiana University has been dedicated to the proposition that the natural academic home for philanthropic studies is a school of liberal arts. The curricula of most of the several hundred philanthropy programs around the United States are grounded in fundraising and non-profit management. While these subjects also represent an important part of the curriculum at Indiana, our program provides students with substantial doses of coursework outside the usual fundraising and management models. This curriculum includes both required and elective courses in philosophy, religion, literature, and history, among other liberal arts disciplines. Such courses are predicated on the judgment that careful reading and discussion of classic texts in our intellectual tradition can illuminate contemporary philanthropic practice, and do so very effectively.

When such textual encounters take place in the company of other committed learners, they can enrich who we are and how we act. Unless we understand who we are, what we are about, and how we came to be ourselves, our philanthropic excellence is likely to be needlessly constrained. Such an approach to the study of philanthropy contrasts sharply with what might be called a behaviorist approach. A behaviorist approach says that if we simply get people involved at an early stage of life in giving and volunteering, the momentum they establish will carry them onward in the same direction. While there is little doubt that the habits we develop powerfully shape every aspect of our lives, understanding plays an equal and in some ways more vital role in shaping how we give.

We cannot make ourselves or anyone else truly generous through external manipulation. If we are to become the most giving people possible, it is vital that we engage our deepest aspirations. If we do so, we are capable of transcending ourselves, of becoming more than we are. In the quest to achieve such a transformation, reading great books is valuable and for some of us necessary. Why? Because our character, our moral compass, and our vision of the good are all powerfully shaped by the stories we hear and tell. We can talk indefinitely about the rules and regulations that philanthropic organizations and their agents must abide by, but ultimately every such organization is defined by the human beings that make it up. Who are those human beings? What draws them to giving and sustains them in their philanthropic endeavors?

One of the greatest philosophical and literary explorations of the human soul ever composed is Plato's *Republic,* written in Athens in the fourth century BC. Its title in Greek is the *Politiea,* usually rendered in English as the *Republic.* Other European tongues often render it as the *State.* Both translations are misleading, as the dialogue deals with much more than just a system of government. It concerns itself with numerous extra-governmental issues, including child rearing, goodness, and the sacred. The dialogue appears to be about justice, but the Greek term usually translated as "justice" encompasses more. *Dikaisyne* means not merely what the law says or what a principle of fairness dictates, but our full range of aspirations for living together in community. These far-reaching implications disturbed twentieth-century philosopher Karl Popper. In his book *The Open Society and Its Enemies,* Popper attacks the *Republic* as a blueprint for the modern totalitarian state.

Others, however, read Plato's masterpiece not as a blueprint for a new society, but as a thought experiment, focused less on the strengths of justice than on its weaknesses as the sole principle for organizing a community. In the dialogue, justice is variously defined as paying our debts, doing good to friends and harm to enemies, minding our own business, respecting the will of the stronger, creating a social contract that protects the weak from the strong, and doing what we are best suited for. At every point, however, Socrates, Plato's favorite character, hints that the human soul aspires to more. It needs more than mere guidance. It needs inspiration. We recognize that liberty is an essential ingredient in the recipe for a full human life, but liberty alone is not enough. As Isaiah Berlin argued, we want freedom as in "freedom from"—the freedom to lead lives free of coercion—but we also want freedom as in "freedom for"—the freedom to devote our lives to purposes larger than ourselves.

Socrates explores the connection between individual human beings and the communities they inhabit. He regards the stories and myths to which we are exposed in youth as vitally important, so important, in fact, he argues that the community must exercise censorship over them. For example, young people should never be exposed to stories that show just men as unhappy or happy men as unjust. Likewise, stories that show the gods in conflict with one another or acting ignobly should be forbidden. The only models of conduct young people encounter must be righteous and noble.

Of course there are problems with Socrates' suggestion, problems of which he himself is keenly aware. If we rewrite poetry to make it conform to justice, will it still engage the human heart? Will sacred texts rewritten to make them conform to justice still engage the human soul? Probably not. Why? Inner psychological tension and unmet longing are crucial engines that propel a Greek tragedy or a Shakespeare play. The conflict between noble and ignoble motives and the development of moral insight are integral to the development of biblical characters such as Jacob and David. If we reduce our stories and myths to mere museums of virtuous character, we will be like physicians who direct all their attention to controlling weight, blood pressure, and serum triglyceride levels, but know nothing of any larger vision of health and flourishing.

After Socrates, the *Republic*'s most important character is one of Plato's brothers, the immensely gifted Glaucon. Early in the dialogue, Socrates paints an initial portrait of a good community, against which Glaucon immediately rebels. Why? Because it is a city of mere efficiency, constructed around meeting the most basic human needs for food, clothing, and shelter. Its design is clever because the division of labor permits a much higher degree of productivity than would be possible if everyone had to grow their own food, make their own clothes, and build their own houses. Yet Glaucon cannot imagine living there. It is a community that lacks what he calls "relishes." He calls it a "city of sows." Glaucon rightly sees that a community that concerns itself only with providing for basic human needs is little more than a farm whose inmates happen to be people instead of livestock.

To lead truly human lives, we need much more than food, clothing, and shelter. What we need, Glaucon recognizes, is inspiration. We need something higher and better than our bellies to live for. Socrates' first portrait of a just community is a challenge. Glaucon rises to that challenge in recognizing that human beings are meant for better things. He demands of Socrates a different, more complex account of human beings and our communities, one that includes our capacities to dream and to make our dreams a reality. Socrates' challenge is directed not only to Glaucon, but to us, the dialogue's readers, as well. What do we dream of? Specifically, what sort of philanthropy do we envision, and what do we dare to hope that our generosity might accomplish? It is, after all, an expression of hope. Physicians do not merely cure patients, they also help to shape our hopes, even when no cure is possible or even needed. Similarly, philanthropists not only fill empty bellies and put roofs over heads—they also embody a vision of human good.

Socrates goes on to construct what he calls a "perfectly just city." It is an incredible place, where "thought police" control what people see and hear, "noble lies" are told to keep people in line, the government controls mating, and parents and children do not know one another. To achieve a perfectly just community, in other words, it is necessary to do away with desire, both our natural attraction to other people and our desire to transcend our circumstances. Our deep desire for our own, as manifested in family life and our hope for a better life for our children, is simply set aside. Perfect social harmony requires psychic castration, a sterilization of the imagination. Socrates clearly recognizes the impracticality of such a community. To create it, he says, would require that everyone over the age of ten years be expelled. Moreover, the eugenics program mandates a degree of control over breeding that is unattainable. As a result, the perfectly just city can never come into being.

In pointing out the essential inhumanity of perfect justice, Socrates invites us to critique the view of the human soul on which it depends. It is an incomplete and hence profoundly unbalanced vision. In magnifying justice out of all proportion, it minifies love to the point of invisibility. Justice alone, though necessary, is sterile. Only love is generative. If justice means keeping everything and everyone in its place, then love represents the aspiration to a new and better place. In Socrates' first account of the human soul, he describes three parts: reason, spirit, and desire. By the end of the *Republic,* he has revised the constituents of this tripartite structure in a subtle but profound way. Reason, spirit, and desire are replaced by the wisdom-loving, victory-loving, and gain-loving parts. A model of the soul that once included love as but one of three parts has now become completely suffused with love. Every part is a loving part.

As we progress through the argument of the *Republic,* we discover that the best human community is not one that eradicates desire. The best human community is one that educates desire. Without love, giving can never rise above mere justice. Without love, it is a mere exercise in mathematics, the attempt to achieve a certain balance or proportion between haves and have-nots. It aims at nothing more than redistribution. In fact, however, love is the best impetus of human giving, without which it cannot achieve its fullest expression. Its two great excellences are hope and generosity. Giving at its best requires the recognition that life could be better, the imagination necessary to develop a vision of what such a better life would look like, the inspiration to pursue that vision, and the know-how to bring it about in practice. On this account, love and desire are not bad. In fact, we cannot hope to be our best without them.

Though Socrates sings the praises of mathematics as a means of training the mind, he repeatedly criticizes a purely quantitative approach to soul craft. In critiquing the eugenics program of the "perfectly just city," he cites the rulers' inability to find the "marriage number" that would provide complete order to mating. No mathematical principle, in other words, can regulate human love and affection. Likewise, in describing the superiority of the philosopher's life to that of the tyrant, Socrates states that the philosopher lives "729 times more pleasantly." His point is not that we should check his figures, but that the very effort to "figure it out," that is, to quantify the worth of one life compared to another, is misguided. Justice can work by mathematical proportions, but love cannot. We simply cannot quantify what we mean to each other.

The *Republic* is all about education. How should we educate ourselves so that we can develop into the most complete human beings we are capable of being? Compare this aspiration with some of the major themes in current educational discourse. What are we trying to do? In large part, we are trying to ensure that our educational resources are used as efficiently as possible. How do we assess efficiency? According to such parameters as test scores and graduation rates. There are several dangers in such an approach. For one thing, we cannot quantify many of our most important educational objectives, such as producing liberally educated human beings. Furthermore, our proxies of success, such as test scores, tend to become idols in their own right. Soon we are teaching not to a vision of a well-educated human being, but to the tests. And if the tests do not measure something, such as the capacity to appreciate a great poem or piece of music, then we may soon find that this capacity has disappeared from our curriculum.

Something similar can happen in philanthropy. To promote greater accountability, we develop "dashboards" for philanthropic organizations, a collection of gauges or metrics by which to evaluate their performance. Naturally, we are drawn to measurable parameters. These include revenue, expenses, fundraising and administrative costs, and working capital ratio, as well as the rate of change in these parameters over time. Our principal data source becomes the IRS Form 990, the financial report non-profits are required to file with the Internal Revenue Service. There is nothing wrong with measuring how much money we give and how well it is used by the organizations to which we give it. There is, however, something wrong when we begin driving with our eyes glued to the instrument panel.

Like Socrates' "perfectly just city," philanthropic organizations that focus excessively on efficiency are liable to develop inspirational deficit disorder. A dashboard of strictly financial gauges provides insufficient information and perspective to navigate a philanthropic organization effectively. No one wants to give to a wasteful organization. No one wants to be involved with organizations whose staff members are using resources inappropriately. Yet efficiency and non-maleficence are not the highest and best goods to which philanthropy can aspire. If we are not careful, we may allow efficiency and the fear of failure to so dominate our thinking that we no longer take risks or innovate. The safest place for a ship may be the harbor, but a ship that never leaves the harbor is a ship in name only. To what great things do we aspire?

Here is where stories and myths, what Plato refers to in the *Republic* as poetry, are positively vital. Our hopes and dreams ultimately define our philanthropic organizations. A perfectly just philanthropic organization may score perfectly on all the quantitative gauges yet accomplish very little of worth in the community and provide a thoroughly uninspiring place for people to work. There are many important truths expressible in stories and myths that mathematics and even philosophical arguments cannot capture. Socrates is not urging us to give up our attempts to figure out the world. Instead he is reminding us that everything worth saying cannot be rendered in figures. Confronted with his vision of people whose hearts have been cut out to serve their heads, we recognize that heartless human beings are not really human. Heartless philanthropy is no less oxymoronic.

Justice is the lowest common denominator of human virtues. In a negative sense, it describes what we ought not do to one another. In its positive sense, it describes what each of us has a right to expect from others. It is the principle that shapes many of our laws, such as prohibitions against fraud, theft, and murder. In an unjust world, other virtues such as generosity become more difficult or even impossible to practice. It is hard to care for others we think are trying to cheat us or steal from us. Yet it is impossible to legislate virtue. We aspire to a higher standard of conduct than merely following the laws. We hope that we will not only refrain from cheating and injuring one another, but also work together for the greater good. We hope that people will not only pay their debts, but also give more than is owed. People of faith do not fully meet their charitable obligations merely by paying their taxes to a welfare state.

What is wrong with a totalitarian state? One problem with the former Soviet Union was the strict limits it placed on human liberty. People were not free to pursue their dreams or to express their ideas.

Even worse, however, the state presumed to provide for every human need. It aspired to true totalitarianism, because everything was meant to be under the state's control—not only the means of production, but the obligation to care for the needy. Philanthropy and generosity were effectively outlawed. To say that people's needs were not being met constituted an implicit criticism of the state. Only a defective state could permit the existence of poverty, homelessness, illiteracy, and the other forms of deprivation to which philanthropy responds. To point out such defects by setting up a charitable organization independent of the state would have been regarded as an act of treason.

Even the most just of totalitarian states is doomed from the outset. It constrains the freedom of thought and expression on which a truly vibrant and creative community depends. It tells us what role we are to play rather than letting us discover for ourselves. As a result, it misallocates its most precious resource, its people. In the long run, it cannot compete scientifically, technologically, culturally, or economically with societies where freedom reigns. Still worse, even the most just of totalitarian states constrains the pursuit of human excellence. If we cannot think for ourselves, we cannot think very well, and thus cannot flourish fully as human beings. We are treated like children our whole lives. It is impossible to be our best when someone is dangling the jailor's key before us, telling us what we must do.

A constant threat of punishment is harmful to character. It does not foster integrity. If we are told that we should avoid injustice because any unjust act will be detected and punished, then we will naturally doubt that justice could possibly be its own reward. It implies that we are expected to do things that our characters alone would not lead us to do. Where the people are just, the threat of punishment is unnecessary. Where the threat of punishment is constant, justice cannot flourish. We would not be acting of our own volition. We would feel dominated and oppressed, and resentment would build. Imagine a world in which every time children performed a generous act, a parent or teacher said, "It is a good thing you did that, because had you done otherwise, you would have received a beating." How generous would such children become?

Good government is a largely necessary but far from sufficient condition for human flourishing, including the flourishing of essential human excellences such as generosity. It is difficult to be a good person under a corrupt and intrusive regime. Likewise, it is difficult to create a good government without good people to constitute it. Yet it is not impossible. Some of the world's greatest works of literature and philosophy were written under tyrannies, some of our best governments were born of rebellion against oppression, and some of our wisest prophets have found their voice while laboring under unjust conditions.

As Aristotle points out in his *Politics,* we need things we can call our own in order to have the means to be generous. If nothing belongs to us, then we have nothing we can choose to share. In a communist state, it is impossible to be generous with our treasure. In a totalitarian state, it is impossible to be generous with our time and talent, as well. Only if what we have is ours and if we are free to choose not to share it are we capable of true generosity.

Toward the end of the *Republic,* Socrates again sharply criticizes poetry and mythmaking. He criticizes them because they appeal to the lowest parts of the soul, which must be shaped by reason if we are to lead fully human lives. He is really saying, however, that the stories and myths we tell have an immense effect on us. From civilization-defining works such as the Homeric epics and the Bible to our private and often unarticulated fantasy lives, these stories make us who we are. We need to attend to them closely.

There is deep irony in Socrates' banishment of the poets, because as soon as he finishes pronouncing it, he immediately begins making a myth of his own. This tale is the myth of Er, a beautifully imaginative account of life after death, where good people are rewarded and wicked people punished. Despite Plato's feud with the poets, his dialogues are nothing if not poetic. The lesson for philanthropic organizations is this: Stories are the lifeblood of our organizations. It is above all in stories that we find inspiration, and it is by sharing our very best stories that we can achieve our full philanthropic potential.

20

SUFFERING

Natalie was fifteen years old when she died. Numerous photographs before she fell ill show a somewhat short, slightly stout teenager whose toothy smile exudes great enthusiasm. Natalie was a natural leader who played on her high school's softball and volleyball teams and participated enthusiastically in her local 4-H chapter. The year before her death, in fact, she had won the Grand Champion prize at the county fair for her favorite steer. She was a member of her local Youth for Christ organization and Bible Club and played an active role in the youth group of her Methodist church. On the date she would have celebrated her sixteenth birthday, her four best friends organized a game day at the local fire station, during which dozens of family members and friends gathered to play board games, eat pizza, and remember Natalie.

She fell ill around Christmas time. Like other teenagers, she had suffered pain in her knees off and on for several years. One day, however, the pain awakened her from sleep. Her mother took her to the emergency room, where the physician ordered blood tests, which showed that she was severely anemic. A bone marrow biopsy was performed, which demonstrated that her bones were packed with abnormal small, round, blue cells. She was referred to the children's hospital at the state's university medical center, where a CT scan showed a mass in her pelvis and multiple abnormally enlarged lymph nodes. A biopsy of one of these lesions proved that she was suffering from rhabdomyosarcoma, a malignant tumor that arises from muscle cells. The malignant tissue in the lymph nodes proved that the tumor had already spread to other parts of her body.

In hopes of shrinking the tumor, Natalie was placed on an aggressive chemotherapy regimen. Follow-up CT and MR scans were performed to assess the tumor's response. Unfortunately, the scans showed that the mass in her pelvis was not shrinking. In fact, the tumor-containing lymph nodes were actually growing. Her doctors tried different chemotherapy regimens, but each time the tumor failed to respond. The lesions would stop growing for a time, but they never shrank, and before long they would expand again. Eventually, the tumor extended its reach to other parts of her body, such as her lungs. Over the eight months between diagnosis and death, Natalie grew progressively thinner and weaker. Because of the pain she was experiencing and the effect of the treatment on her immune system, she was unable to attend school. Fortunately, her teachers were willing to visit her home to teach her.

In the warmest months of the following summer, it became clear that Natalie was declining fast. She could no longer eat and would not even look at her favorite food, baked potatoes. Her oncologist told the family that she would probably live only a matter of weeks. The Make-a-Wish Foundation had recently contacted the family, and Natalie requested for her special wish that they remodel and refurnish her bedroom. Knowing that her sister, with whom she shared the room, would be the only one using it in the coming years, Natalie made sure she was very involved in the planning. Many family members and friends transformed her bedroom into a palace, in which everything, including the carpet, walls, furniture, shelves, and even television set were painted Natalie's favorite colors: purple, lime green, and blue. A week later, having grown so sick that she refused even to take sips of ice water, Natalie died at home in her new purple bed.

Six months later, Natalie's mother and aunt talked with me about her illness. They did so without even a hint of bitterness.

"Was Natalie angry about what happened to her?" I asked. "After all, she was a vibrant young girl, everybody's best friend, with so much going on in her life. Then abruptly, out of the blue, she is stricken with a terrible cancer that fails to respond to any treatment."

"No," her mother responded. "Natalie never got down about it. She believed that what was happening to her was God's will, that God had a plan for her."

"What about you?" I asked. "How are you coping?"

"Of course we miss her, but we are not angry. Who would we be angry at? We are sorry she got sick, but we believe that Natalie is now in a better place, with God. We know that she is happy and whole there, and that she is waiting for us to join her."

"I don't see how you can avoid feeling cheated."

"If you thought this is the only life we had," continued Natalie's mother, "you might get depressed or angry, but when you know that there is a better life ahead, you are just glad that Natalie's suffering is over."

"It is amazing to me that you are so at peace about it."

"Obsessing over our misfortunes would be selfish. Who ever said that life is just about what I want?"

What would happen if we were unable to suffer? Plato's great dialogue *The Symposium* provides insight into this question. In it, a group of the most powerful and urbane men of Athens join one another for supper, and soon agree that each will offer a speech in praise of love. One of the speeches is by the comic poet Aristophanes, author of such plays as *The Clouds* and *The Frogs*. In his speech, Aristophanes tells a moving tale of how human beings came into being.

Originally, our ancestors were round creatures, resembling two human beings joined together. They were whole, completely self-sufficient, took little interest in one another, and displayed little reverence for the gods. Recognizing that these complete beings represented a threat, the gods decided that they should be severed in two. After the proto-humans were split, the gods drew together the skin of each half at the front of the abdomen at the belly button, which now serves as a reminder of the completeness we once enjoyed. Thereafter, we have carried with us a fleshly reminder of our deep incompleteness. Filled with a desperate longing to be whole again, we spend much of our lives seeking out our other half.

Aristophanes' story illuminates an essential aspect of our humanity: none of us is either complete or self-sufficient. If we are to have any hope of wholeness, we must turn to one another. The wholeness and self-sufficiency of Aristophanes' proto-human creatures rendered them fundamentally inhuman. They were inhuman because they could not know the experience of suffering. They could know no unfulfilled desires.

Aristophanes' proto-humans were locked in a never-ending passionate embrace. They were oblivious to everything else. For them, desire and satisfaction were essentially simultaneous. This lack of longing also closed to them the possibility of compassion. How could they feel for the suffering of one another, or of any creature, when they could never know want, privation, and pain themselves? There is something enviable in their wholeness, but also something profoundly cold-blooded and heartless.

In our own age, we expend a great deal of energy and resources in an effort to overcome suffering. We have, for example, carefully studied pain and sought out means of relieving it. Beginning in the middle of the nineteenth century, investigators such as Horace Wells and William Morton began to appreciate the pain-relieving potential of gases such as ether and nitrous oxide, which not only can dull the sense of pain but even render patients completely insensible. Their discoveries ushered in the era of pain-free surgery, and today patients undergo procedures such as dental extractions, appendectomies, and limb amputations without pain.

Such triumphs fostered an expectation that all medical procedures should be painless. Within years, investigators questioned why anesthetic techniques that render surgery pain-free should not be extended to childbirth. Some critics argued that to apply anesthesia to childbirth would be unrighteous. In Genesis, when Adam and Eve are expelled from the Garden of Eden, one of the curses leveled on Eve is that "in sorrow shall you bring forth children." James Simpson, a British obstetrician and pioneer of anesthesia, met this objection with his own scriptural citation. Before the Lord removed a rib from Adam with which to create Eve, Simpson said, he put Adam to sleep. Far from forbidding anesthesia, God was the world's first anesthetist. The popular debate was put quickly to rest when such luminaries as Queen Victoria and Fanny Longfellow gave birth under anesthesia.

Physicians now offer patients not only general inhalation anesthetics such as ether and nitrous oxide, but a vast armamentarium of analgesics, local anesthetics, spinal and nerve blocks, and narcotics. We also have drugs for types of suffering other than pain, such as sedatives, anxiolytics, and a variety of psychoactive preparations to treat behavioral and mood disorders. Pain killers are both licit and illicit, the latter including excessive alcohol consumption, cocaine, and heroin. As our pharmacopoeia expands, some investigators have defined new psychological afflictions, such as social anxiety disorder, a condition in which otherwise normal people feel discomfort when placed in social situations.

Such pharmacological advancements have done a great deal to alleviate human suffering, but they have also caused us to forget some important lessons about what it means to be human. Even if we could relieve all the pain of injuries and diseases, human beings would still suffer. Why? Because our suffering is rooted not only in our afflictions, but also in our appetites. As Plato indicated, we suffer in part because our dreams and desires exceed our grasp. We are able to imagine things that we cannot bring to pass. Part of this suffering arises from competition, which gives rise to envy. Though we have enough to be happy, our neighbor's surplus makes us feel that we need more. Yet envy is only part of the whole story. The sense of privation is also rooted in the very possibility of aspiration. If we ever gained everything we desire, what would we have left to live for?

As our power to combat some forms of suffering has grown, our intolerance toward it has expanded apace. When we go to the dentist to have a cavity filled, or into the hospital for an operation, we expect to be spared any pain. When we go to the doctor complaining of a headache or a toothache, we expect to get relief. In some well-publicized cases, rich and famous people have succumbed to the temptation to go from doctor to doctor in search of drugs to ease their suffering. As a result, they have become addicted to painkillers. Suffering no longer seems intrinsic to human existence. Instead it appears a nuisance, like a pesky fly that we expect to shoo away.

Our tolerance for the sufferings of others has also diminished. Most of us no longer expect to encounter suffering in our daily lives. It would strike us as out of place to be approached on the street by someone naked, homeless, hungry, sick, or under threat of physical violence. We have removed the sick and dying to hospitals, found ways to mask the strangeness of people suffering from mental illness, and segregated our cities so that the comfortably well off need only rarely bump into the dispossessed. Suffering has become tinged with shame. Just as we feel shame in being asked for help, we feel ashamed to meet people who plainly could use it.

We also experience discomfort or even anger toward the suffering. When we meet someone in distress, it calls to mind the fragility of our own well-being. It reminds us that we too are vulnerable. We too could be reduced to a position of dependence. Any day, we could feel a lump under our armpit, see blood in our urine, or find our face or arm gone suddenly weak. No one is completely safe, a fact about which we would prefer not to be reminded.

Would the world be a better place if we could expunge suffering completely? Not likely. A life devoid of the possibility of suffering would be a life devoid of appetite. No privation would mean no want, and a being without desire would be no human being at all. To live without desire would require a permanent state of unconsciousness, or at least idiocy. We dare not grow sick of suffering, nor even our liability to it. Such an aspiration is dehumanizing. Such sterility would protect us in some ways, but deaden us in others.

Do we need to suffer? Do we require suffering to become complete human beings? Is suffering a vital ingredient in the recipe for our fruition and ripening, like the trials through which a group of soldiers are put to become a true fighting unit? This is a difficult question. Certainly suffering may have benefits. Plato's account reminds us that a complete imperviousness to suffering would take a severe toll on our capacity for compassion. Someone who had never known the sensation of hunger would have difficulty understanding what it means to be hungry. Someone who had never felt pain would have difficulty responding appropriately to another's injury. Someone who had never closed his eyes would find it difficult to understand blindness. It is through our own suffering that we gain the capacity to recognize and respond to the afflictions of others.

More broadly speaking, suffering helps us to recognize our own vulnerability, the fact that every human being is to some degree insecure. None of us, no matter what our station in life, is completely impervious to hunger, cold, and pain. We are not different from the afflicted. Far from it, we are the afflicted. We share the same human liabilities, from which no creed, race, nationality, language, or degree of wealth can inure us.

A key component of suffering is uncertainty, the fact that we never know for sure what lies ahead. Every decision we make is uncertain to some degree. If we begin to proceed otherwise, we are liable to act foolishly.

Is our capacity for suffering a feature of our evolutionary heritage? If we could not know hunger, our species would have died out long ago, our forebears having starved to death. If contact with fire did not burn, we would have gone up in flames. There is a very rare and fascinating medical condition called congenital insensitivity to pain. Individuals with this condition frequently become scarred and disabled because they do not refrain from activities that should hurt.

The capacity for suffering is not merely the product of a struggle to survive, but a necessary condition of our flourishing. If we could not suffer, we could not become complete human beings, able to respond compassionately to the afflictions of others and capable of exhibiting courage in the face of danger. The immortal gods of the Homeric epics do not have so much at stake. As a result, they lead lives that seem vain and superficial in comparison to the mortal heroes.

Suffering is integral to the courage of love. When we love someone, it is as though we extend our skin around them. We assume, or at least share, their liabilities. When misfortune befalls our spouse, our child, our parent, our sibling, or our friend, we suffer too. When they fall ill, our world is also turned upside down. When they are disappointed in love or in life, we too shed a tear. In loving, we open ourselves up, expose ourselves to the slings and arrows of others' fortunes. It might be safer to keep ourselves shut off, to remain behind the walls, basking in our own security. But that would land us back among Plato's round creatures, shielded but also completely cut off from those we should be turning to. Such isolation is not fit for loving and lovable—and therefore incomplete—human beings.

Should we then seek out suffering? When an infection develops, should we withhold antibiotics? When cancer is diagnosed, should we refrain from surgically removing it? Of course not. Throughout much of the eighteenth century, dental caries and gingivitis were so widespread that everyone seemed to spend a good part of his or her life moaning of toothache. Only a masochist could long for such times. Yet in saying that it would be irrational to seek out suffering for its own sake, we do not commit ourselves to preventing or alleviating all forms of it. Bereavement is an appropriate reaction to the death of a loved one. Heartache is an appropriate reaction to the end of a deep relationship. Simply taking pills to make those feelings go away turns us into something less than we are.

How should we understand suffering and live in light of it? For one thing, we need to recognize that it is part of our cultural and linguistic heritage, as well as our biological endowment. Every time we suffer, we do so within a larger context of meaning. The same symptom, a pain in the calf, might be interpreted very differently by different people in different cultures. One might explain it as growing pains. Another might account for it in terms of a humoral imbalance. Another might see in it evidence of a blood clot in a vein. Still another might ascribe the pain to a curse.

Even in our own culture, suffering is handled very differently. When intravenous drug users present with a blood infection from using dirty needles, one hospital staff member may hurl epithets such as "dirtball" at them for jeopardizing their health. By contrast, another staff member who knows such patients' social backgrounds and life histories might see the same circumstances as a summons to compassion.

To assert that there are different ways of understanding suffering is not to grant that all are equal. Nineteenth- and twentieth-century microbiology afforded us diagnostic and therapeutic options unknown to the ancient physicians. It also offered advantages over accounts that treated fever as the manifestation of a transgression against divine law.

Yet biomedical science is not the only available point of view. If viewing suffering in strictly molecular terms requires us to blind ourselves to the human meaning of suffering, then we need to rethink our explanation. If our science leads us to regard the patient's reaction to pain as unreal or insignificant, then it is leading us astray. All the science in the world is not sufficient if it prevents us from being there for someone who needs us. Compassion is not the only standard by which to judge explanations of suffering, but our attention should never stray far from it.

What do we need to do? First, we need to seek out opportunities to enrich our understanding in ways that make us more responsive to suffering. We should be wary of explanations that draw sharp distinctions between those who suffer and those who do not. Both sufferers and those who care for them, or fail to care for them, are made of the same perishable substance. When we see people in desperate straits, it is better to think, "There but for the grace of God go I" rather than "Thank God I am not like them."

Rather than flee from suffering, we should enhance our sensitivity to it. Rather than ignore the suffering around us, we should recognize it and allow its claim to get under our skin. To be sure, compassion can be subject to abuse. Occasional whiners and malingerers may seek to exploit it. Yet is compassion not better than a cold heart?

No one would pray to suffer. It is not wrong to pray that we be spared suffering. When such trials arise, we naturally long for their passing. Yet it is unreasonable to pray never to suffer. Answering such a prayer would cut us off from one another. Insulating us would stifle our humanity. Instead we should pray to bear it as well as we can. We should cope with it bravely, with as much dignity as we can muster. Our response can guide others, serving as a touchstone when similar trials befall them. We should also pray to learn as much as we can from suffering. What is really most important to us in life? What do we really need? Who are we? These rank among the very most important discoveries we can hope to make in life.

When someone close to us suffers and dies, there is a possibility that it really is God's will. We know what such events mean to us, but we cannot be certain what it means from a larger, divine perspective. It is entirely possible that we do not fathom the true meaning. Compared to God, we may be like insects buzzing around a porch light, with only the dimmest notion of what is really going on inside the house. None of us is fit to serve as creator and sustainer of the universe. Would the world truly be a better place if all our life's wishes had been granted? Are we equipped to take the reins of creation? Perhaps we are limited even in our ability to craft our own happiness, let alone the flourishing of the universe.

Could it be that the most appropriate attitude toward suffering is a tragic one? Tragic not in the sense of defeatist or nihilistic, but as the ancient Greek tragedians Aeschylus and Sophocles intended.

A tragic sense of life is not so different from a religious one. In both cases, we recognize significances in life that we do not grasp. Not only do things happen for reasons that we cannot discern, but our very ability to describe what is happening is severely limited in a number of respects. Do we know enough to object to the pattern in which creation is unfolding? All we really know is that events sometimes hurt us deeply. We need not pretend that they feel good, but dare we blame God for permitting them?

The mystery of suffering serves as a powerful reminder of another deep mystery at the heart of humanity. Creation is not ordered solely to our understanding, convenience, or enjoyment. Its purposes exceed even our ken, let alone our control. Just because we cannot explain a terrible event, we must not conclude that God is evil or does not care. We are, after all, not created as gods. We are created as human beings, and we must recognize the limitations of being human. These limitations are every bit as integral to our flourishing as our capabilities. We are not round creatures, completely self-sufficient, whole, and invulnerable. We are incomplete, sometimes even broken creatures, and it is in knowing our brokenness and incompleteness that we glimpse our place in the larger scheme of things.

As I finished my conversation with Natalie's mother and aunt, I asked them whether anything good had come from Natalie's illness and death.

"Yes, I think so," said her aunt. "Her friends' priorities have been changed. They spend less time arguing with one another and worrying about material things. It also brought out in all of us things we didn't know were there. Coming out to the house after school to teach Natalie taught her teachers what it really means to care for a student. It also brought the people of our county together. By the end, everyone knew Natalie and what she had been through."

"Do you suppose," asked her mother, "that learning about Natalie's experience could help people become better at caring for those in need?"

21

TREASURE IN EARTHEN VESSELS

The circumstances of my first encounter with the family seemed un-remarkable. A colleague of mine approached me to assist in placing a patient's gastrojejunostomy tube. Such a tube enters the stomach through a hole in the skin of the abdomen. It enables liquid food, medications, and water to be infused directly into the intestines, by-passing the mouth, throat, esophagus, and stomach. This is necessary in patients who cannot swallow, those with swallowing impairments who tend to aspirate food into their lungs, and those with severe re-flux of stomach contents back up into their throats.

The patient in question was a fourteen-year-old boy named David. He was accompanied by his parents, Patty and Ron. Patty insisted that he receive a new feeding tube. The relatively skinny feeding tubes we had been placing (three times in the past two weeks, as it turned out) were becoming clogged frequently. Each time this oc-curred, a new tube had to be placed. This meant that David had to be transported by ambulance to the hospital by two paramedics, a time-consuming and expensive process. Moreover, each time the tube clogged, he had begun to suffer leakage of acidic stomach se-cretions around it, which was damaging his skin.

I entered the room to speak with his mother. On the fluoroscopy table lay a fourteen-year-old boy who was about the size of a ten-year-old. I immediately surmised that he had been adopted. For one thing, he was black and his parents were white. Moreover, Patty and Ron seemed too advanced in years to be his biological parents. David's arms and legs were thin and contorted, and he stared blankly off into space. He was obviously neurologically devastated, and he was connected to a machine that helped him breathe. At his side, Patty wore a sweatshirt that bore the message, "Count your blessings." She looked like someone who had not slept for several days. I introduced myself and asked her to explain the situation. She answered politely, but could not hide her frustration. As she recounted their recent difficulties, she reached across her son's abdomen and pulled back his dressing, revealing a large patch of raw flesh.

He had undergone many abdominal surgeries, and there was little abdominal tissue left to help hold a feeding tube in place. The tubes we had been placing for David were about as big around as an adult's ring finger. Because of the leakage, however, the hole was now as big as a middle finger. Simply replacing the tube would allow the leakage to continue, only making things worse. Patty insisted that we find something better for her son, and she would not take no for an answer. We decided to attempt to place a larger tube, which should clog less easily and prevent the leakage. We sent for the tube from the adult hospital. While we waited, a junior colleague and I chatted outside the room.

"That mother is really demanding," he said.

"Yes," I said. "She obviously loves her son a lot."

"Isn't that strange?" he said. "He would have died years ago without someone like her to look after him. He might have been better off."

"What do you mean?" I asked.

"Just look at his quality of life," he responded. "What does he have to live for? He can't breathe on his own or eat on his own, and by the looks of it, he can't communicate in any way. All day he just lies there, doing nothing. He has no clue what is going on around him. I bet he doesn't even know his own mother."

"So?" I asked.

"Well, maybe we aren't doing him any favors by fixing his feeding tube. What if we couldn't get the right tube for him and could no longer put feedings directly into his small intestine? What if the feedings had to be put into his stomach? What if he refluxes and gets pneumonia? And what if we did not treat his pneumonia? Would that be such a bad thing? Who would it hurt if his sufferings finally came to an end?"

Before I had time to answer, the technologist returned with the new feeding tube, which we placed without incident. Inspecting our handiwork, we saw that a tiny gap still persisted around the outer edge of the tube. It was not as wide as before, but until his skin healed, there would still be some leakage. He would require regular dressing changes around the clock to keep his skin clean and dry and permit healing. Some families might balk at such news, but Patty was unfazed. She informed us that she had been getting up with David two or three times a night for many years. Overnight dressing changes would not alter her schedule in any way.

Driving home from the hospital that night, I felt pleased that we had been able to do something for David. Technically, his case seemed a success. If the tube remained clog-free, allowing his skin to heal, he could be fed for years to come. Yet there were important non-technical aspects of the case, to which my colleague had alluded. Were those of us involved in David's care merely prolonging his agony?

In seeking an answer to this question, I arranged to meet David's parents in the hospital cafeteria. As we began to talk, it became clear that Patty and Ron were exceptional people. The parents of six healthy biological children, over the years they had served as foster parents for dozens of others. They had adopted fifteen of these children, all of whom suffered from mental or physical disabilities of some kind. David was one of these children. This only raised more questions. How had they come to be David's parents? Why were they so committed to the care of a child like him? Why did their eyes shine so brightly when they talked about him and his brothers and sisters? Who were Patty and Ron, and what made them tick? We began a series of biweekly conversations that lasted several years, over the course of which their remarkable story unfolded.

Even a cursory inspection of the unfortunate circumstances into which David was born foreshadowed a rocky life. The woman who gave birth to him, Carol, was one of sixteen children. She is mildly mentally retarded. She was fifteen years old when David was born. Patty and Ron describe her as a "warm and sweet person." One of Carol's brothers, David's uncle David, has a more serious mental disability. When David was about a year old and very seriously ill in the hospital, Carol came to visit him. On subsequent visits, she made a point of bringing his Uncle David along. During these visits, her brother would alternately cling to her arm and bat her on the shoulder.

Despite Carol's efforts to hush him, her brother would ask the baby questions like, "When are you going to walk for Daddy?" Once when Patty confronted Carol and her brother about David's paternity, they both just giggled. When David's uncle began to answer, Carol would kick him. When asked if her brother was David's father, she would only respond by saying, "I just can't say that." Patty and Ron think that David's family, and in particular his mother, did not understand that David would never walk or talk. Carol had two more children after David. Both were healthy and performed well in school, at least compared to the rest of the family. When these children were taken away from Carol because of charges of neglect, Patty and Ron felt sorry for her. Patty believes that society was doing Carol no favors by allowing her to have children and then taking them away.

Once when David's siblings were young, about two and a half years and eighteen months old, they had been returned to their mother's care during a late winter cold snap. A few days later, a neighbor called to report that although the children were wearing their coats, they were playing outside without hats and gloves. When a social worker arrived on the scene, she found that the children were not wearing diapers. The social worker took them from Carol's custody. Patty talked at length with Carol, telling her that the children must always wear their diapers. Carol responded, "They screamed to get outside, and I didn't want the neighbors to think I was hitting them." The social worker counseled Carol, and they set up a schedule to make sure the children were fed three times per day and their diapers changed regularly. They even put special markers on a clock to help remind her.

Soon the children were returned to Carol's custody. A week later, however, the police were called back. During a warm spell, when the temperature reached sixty-five degrees, Carol had sent the children out to play all bundled up in their winter coats and snow pants. The little girl had become dehydrated and had passed out in the yard. When David's mother talked again with Carol, she sobbed through her tears, "I am just too stupid to be a mom!"

Patty and Ron were told that David's birth family had the longest record with Child Protective Services of any family in the county. Both David's grandmother and his great grandmother had lost children to foster care. There was never any accusation that the children were beaten or suffered sexual abuse. In each case, the issue was neglect.

Once at a family gathering, two of Carol's brothers had gotten into an argument, and gunshots were fired. Carol never told anyone for fear that her children might be taken away from her. Later in court, fighting to get her children back, Carol said to the judge, "Do you know what it feels like to have everyone tell you how terrible you are, but you feel you're doing a good job?" When David was older, Carol tried a couple of times to help out with his care, but she soon fell ill herself, which was just one more "can't" for her.

Carol never married and worked at a local fast food restaurant for years. She was always clean and well-groomed and always kept her children clean. Because of her mental disability, though, people were always taking advantage of her. For instance, her mother frequently took her food stamps. Carol never reported such incidents for fear it would cause trouble with her children. Patty calls Carol "a real sweetheart."

David seemed normal at birth. Labor and delivery went well, and he fed and gained weight normally. Beginning at two months of age, Carol reported that he had "shaking spells" and took him to the county hospital several times for evaluation. Each time, the doctors could find nothing wrong, and he was released. When David was ten months old, however, his mother handed him to his two-year-old nephew, who promptly dropped him down a flight of stairs. Carol rushed down, and when she reached him, he was shaking. Yet another evaluation at the county hospital proved normal, and he was released to his mother the next day. One month later, the same thing happened—David was handed to his two-year-old nephew, who again dropped him down the stairs. Again he was taken to the hospital. This time, however, his weight was found to have fallen by more than a pound. Carol was told that he would have to be placed in foster care. Another woman became David's foster mother.

In the months that followed, David's foster mother took him to the county hospital three times, asserting that he had a seizure disorder. Each time, however, the doctors saw nothing wrong. It was at this point that Patty and Ron met David for the first time. At the request of a social worker who thought David's foster mother needed a respite, they took him home for a weekend. David was eating normally, playing with toys, and cruising around furniture. Later that weekend, however, David took a dramatic turn for the worse. While eating, he suddenly turned "the bluest I have ever seen." She called 911, and David was transported by ambulance to the children's hospital. While being evaluated, he fell into a grand mal seizure. Despite aggressive treatment, the seizure lasted four and a half hours, and David nearly died.

David spent the next six tumultuous months in the children's hospital. During this time, he suffered three episodes of intussusception, a type of bowel obstruction. He experienced additional bouts of status epilepticus, a severe form of seizure that persists for an extended time despite all therapy. These episodes took a permanent toll on David, and he started to regress developmentally, eventually losing the ability to swallow. It was necessary to insert a feeding tube. He began suffering many seizures each day.

The family had recently lost an adopted child to an irreversible neurologic disorder, and Patty felt reluctant to bring David home. His doctors said he would not live more than a few months. Patty and Ron discussed the situation with their children, who felt they should bring David home. Yet Patty continued to wrestle with the decision. On the one hand, she wanted to care for David. On the other, she feared the pain that another death would cause the family. Sensing that a decision needed to be made, Ron called the caseworker one day and, to the doctors' surprise, made arrangements to bring David home. Despite the expectation that he would die soon, David stopped deteriorating. Before long it became clear that he had reached a plateau and might live for some time. After much discussion, the family decided that David should join them permanently, and he has never left them since.

At the age of three and a half years, David suffered another very severe seizure. Thereafter his stomach no longer functioned properly. Doctors said he would need to have a catheter inserted into one of the veins in his chest so nutrients could be infused directly into his bloodstream. Patty knew that David would eventually develop liver failure and other complications if he were not fed through his intestines. After long debates, a surgeon agreed to attempt to place a gastrojejunostomy tube. During the surgery, David suffered another severe seizure, almost dying. The surgeon came out and told the family that he could not complete the procedure. Patty began to weep and told the surgeon that David had no other option. "We just want to feed our child," she told him. Reluctantly, the surgeon went back into the operating room.

When he came out the second time, he told them the procedure had been successful. However, he also asked David's mother a question: "Did your grandmother ever tell you to be careful what you wish for?" From that point forward, David was fed directly into his intestines. His seizures remained uncontrolled by any medications.

At the age of six and a half years, David developed severe respiratory problems. For two weeks, he lay in a hospital bed, fighting for breath and clutching his chest, a look of terror in his eyes. One day, Patty was feeling particularly exhausted and frustrated. She asked the doctors, "I guess you people in this children's hospital are just going to leave him like this, is that it?" Although another operation posed a significant risk to David's life, they finally agreed to proceed. They would place a tracheostomy tube into his windpipe to ease his breathing, and operate again on his abdomen to relieve yet another bowel obstruction. Once the operation got under way, they found severe scarring in his belly and had to place yet another feeding tube directly into his intestines.

David was very ill after this surgery, and the staff of the intensive care unit (ICU) did not expect him to live. One day, when David's mother was washing him in the ICU, his abdominal incision opened up. The surgeon was called, and he probed the incision with a scalpel. A pocket of pus suddenly opened up with such force that some of it struck the surgeon in the face. At that point the hospital was desperately short of beds, and the surgeon told David's parents that he would need to be moved out of the ICU.

Instead of moving David to another unit in the hospital, Patty and Ron decided that they should simply take David home. David's parents and two home nurses who had once worked in the pediatric ICU cared for him. The nurses gave him a bath every day, "just as though they expected him to get up and go to school." After three and a half months of superb care, his wound finally closed. His doctors expressed amazement that David had once again beaten the odds.

Why did Patty and Ron feel called to care for children with disabilities, children that no one else wanted? Part of the answer lies in their own childhoods. Patty had been one of five children. Her parents divorced when she was an infant, and her mother remarried when Patty was five years old. During her childhood, Patty developed rheumatic fever. This was before the introduction of antibiotics, and she was largely confined to bed for two years. During this time, her stepfather, who was an alcoholic, tried to provide ways for her to escape her boredom and isolation. He would spend hours drawing with her and helping her make up stories. She will never forget the tempura Santa he once painted on her bedroom wall. Her mother often said that she wished she had never had children. She was not a physically warm person, but Patty knows in her heart that she loved her children.

Growing up, Patty's family had been poor, with barely enough money for food and rent. She never really thought about it, though, because she had never known any other life. When she was twelve years old, she suffered a relapse of rheumatic fever and spent another three years on bed rest. Despite the circumstances, she always had the ability to think herself into believing that things were better.

Perhaps because of her own prolonged experiences with illness, as a teenager she wanted to be a nurse. In those days, companies in town offered college scholarships, and she thought she would win one of them. But it turned out that she could not get into nursing school. Because of her history of rheumatic fever, she failed the medical examination,. She felt devastated because she had wanted so badly to be a nurse.

With no other prospects, she went back to high school. Then, in November of her senior year, she met Ron. Both Patty and Ron were lonesome at the time, and theirs was a whirlwind courtship. They were married six weeks later, on Christmas Eve. She went to live with her husband in the military, where he received an extra $60 per month because he had taken a bride.

They both wanted to have a large family. After two months of marriage, Patty went to the doctor to find out why she had not become pregnant. The doctor just howled with laughter. Eventually, six children were born to them. After the sixth child, however, Patty developed myocarditis, an inflammation of the heart muscle, and the doctor told her they could not have more children.

To Ron's mother, his birth seemed a miracle. At the age of forty-two, she had suffered a serious heart attack and had no intention of having more children. Now she was forty-five years old and believed she had already gone through the change of life. She was a short, heavy woman and did not even suspect that she was pregnant until the night before the twins were born.

Though already the mother of six older children, she had lost two babies at birth, both boys. One, who had died from a broken neck during delivery, had reddish hair. The other, who died for no known reason, had a distinctive birthmark on his head. For years, she had grieved over the loss of those two children. Now she found herself going into labor not even suspecting up to that point that she was pregnant.

At delivery, she was amazed to discover that not only had she been pregnant, but that she had been carrying twins. Moreover, one of the boys had reddish hair, and the other had a distinctive birthmark on his head. She always believed that God had given her back the two boys she had lost at birth.

Ron's eyes sparkle when he talks about his childhood. He and his twin brother grew up spoiled. Everyone, including his parents and older siblings, always doted over them. Their oldest brothers and sisters already had families of their own, and he and his twin frequently traveled with them on vacations.

Though the family was of modest means, the two boys rarely did without things they wanted. He says that his childhood couldn't have been better even if they had been millionaires. In those days, parents thought nothing of allowing their children to ride off on their bicycles for the entire day, and the boys would frequently go out on excursions to a reservoir about ten miles away to fish.

Ron was small, but he was good at sports, and this helped him develop into a neighborhood leader. He recalls that he and his friends pulled their share of youthful pranks, including egging cars in the neighborhood and once putting girls' underpants on the steering wheel of their preacher's car.

Ron's parents were unusual people. His mother came from a family of twelve children and his father from a family of eight. As their family grew and his older brothers and sisters began to get married and start families of their own, his father built a three-car garage behind their house. Once the garage was complete, his parents, he, and his brother moved into the garage, and the older children lived in the house. Throughout his childhood, even after some of his older brothers and sisters had moved into houses of their own, they still came by every morning for breakfast and to drop off their laundry.

The family was very involved in church, which they attended several times per week, and their father was always doing carpentry and other projects there. The children grew up believing that God was right there with them. Ron remembers thinking that learning about God was fun, and most of the children looked forward to spending a morning at church, complete with a pancake breakfast.

His father frequently talked about religion and the priorities their family should have in life. He always said that you should put God first, family second, and self last. His mother spoke less about these matters, but he always felt that his parents complemented each other well. He says now that his father said a lot and his mother showed a lot.

Ron's father was a large man, standing six feet five inches tall. He worked as a bus driver. Ron remembers him as a disciplinarian, though he was only spanked three times in his entire childhood. On one of these occasions, when he was older, his mother spanked him first, and he laughed at her. When his father got home, however, he got another spanking, and after that he wasn't laughing anymore.

Despite the pain, he reports that he always preferred spanking over his father's usual means of discipline, which was to give the offender a good talking to. He respected his father so much that he suffered more from disappointing him than anything else.

His father was strict in his religious observance and tithed 10 percent of his income every week. When his own mother fell ill, he visited her religiously every day after work. He used to say that his day had to become two hours longer because he needed to go visit Grandma. Though he could be stern, he was also one of the most jovial people Patty and Ron have ever known. His laugh was like a roar that would shake the whole house.

Ron remembers his mother rising at three o'clock each morning to start cooking. Every day she would make eggs, bacon, fried potatoes, pork chops, biscuits, and coffee, and the whole family would converge on the house for breakfast. She also did the laundry for the whole family, even after most of the children were grown. She had an old wringer washer, and she always ironed everything, singing the whole time. Ron remembers when she finally got an electric washer. She beamed with almost regal pride.

Though the family had a car, they always walked everywhere. His mother never failed to have her hair done each week at a downtown department store. Though his mother bore the lion's share of the cooking, cleaning, and childcare responsibilities, his mother and father had a relationship that made it clear that in their minds, as Patty puts it, "God does not wear curlers."

The kids in the neighborhood called his father "Mister," but everyone called his mother "Mom." At any one time, three to five kids from the neighborhood would be staying in their home, occasionally for a few weeks at a time. Their house was considered a neighborhood refuge.

He remembers one family who lived about three blocks away. The mother and father were alcoholics, and the children were always dirty. From time to time, their parents would throw them out, and they would come and spend a week or two at his home. Everyone in the family took this completely in stride, and it seemed natural to him growing up that kids from other families would come and stay with them.

One of the kids would simply say, "Mom, Cecil needs to spend a couple three days with us," to which their mother would say, "Okay, but he has to go to school. I'll make up a palette."

Some of these neighborhood children were known to be infested with lice, but the family never begrudged them a place to stay. Once the children had gone back to their home, his mother would simply have the house fumigated. Patty once asked her, "Why did you take those children in, knowing you would have to fumigate?" She responded, "Where did that question come from? Not the heart!"

Ron's mother and father were not without their faults. For example, they were strongly opposed to racial integration. When Patty and Ron became foster parents of a black child, they feared that his father would be angry. By that point, he was about seventy years old. They did not tell him about it in advance, however, and simply showed up at the next family gathering with the little girl.

At first, he was standoffish. He said, "I see you have a new one." Ron said, "Yes, Dad, and we are going to keep her." To Patty's mind, the thing that really broke the ice was that the baby was handicapped. Once Dad realized this, any animosity the baby's new grandfather might have felt immediately diffused. Within half an hour, he had the little girl on his lap, and after that, race was never an issue for anyone else in the family.

Patty describes the day Mom died as the worst day of her life, because she meant so much to everyone. She never held a job, though hers was not a life of leisure. She never did things to draw attention to herself in the community, but she was known by everyone. When she died at the age of sixty-two, her funeral was the largest the funeral home had ever seen. They had to open up three rooms just to hold all the flowers sent in her memory, and it was estimated that there were 350 cars in her funeral procession.

Mom has been gone for many years, but Patty says she feels she is still with them every day of their life. To her mind, Ron combines his father's strong sense of direction with his mother's soft-teddy-bear hug. She says that his family still laughs more and loves more than any family she has ever experienced.

David was neither the first nor the only child Patty and Ron adopted. They had six birth children at the time they become interested in welcoming more children into their family. Their pastor at church had already adopted two children, including one Vietnamese orphan. Another couple had decided that they, too, would adopt a Vietnamese child. But when they found that the baby's hair was curly, which meant that the father was black, they pulled out. Patty and Ron had considered adoption in the past, and when they learned of this little Vietnamese girl's plight, they decided they would adopt her.

At this time, their youngest child was five years old, and David had not been born yet. Three planes were scheduled to fly out of Vietnam, and their little girl was on the first one, which carried approximately eighty-five children and medical staff members. However, as the plane was leaving the country, it was shot down. The little girl and all the other children waiting to be adopted were killed.

David's parents were deeply saddened. The caseworker who had helped them with the adoption told them they could still adopt. In fact, she told them, there were thousands of children in the United States at that moment who did not have a home. This convinced them to adopt a child from the United States.

They did have stipulations, however. They told the caseworker that they did not want to adopt a child with any "uncorrectable" problems. They felt that taking on a child who would be handicapped for the rest of his or her life would be a mistake because they did not want to subject their birth children to that.

Their first adopted child was four months old when they received her. At the time, they were told that she was partially deaf, but that this could be corrected with hearing aids. In time, it turned out that the child was not deaf, but mentally retarded.

This first child was black. While their friends could see that Patty and Ron loved their children, they were concerned that bringing home a child of a different race might cause trouble in their neighborhood. Patty and Ron were active in the neighborhood Presbyterian Church, and Ron was a leader of the Boy Scout troop that met in the church basement. They made it clear that they were not trying to save the world or to convince others that they were wrong. They were just trying to help a child in need.

They were very close to their neighbors. Yet not everyone agreed with the family's decision to adopt a child of a different race. One night their house burned down, and the police said that the fire had been set intentionally. They faced a difficult decision: Should they stay in the neighborhood or move away? After long discussions, they decided to stay. Before long, however, their garage was also torched. After the fire had been put out, they found a racial epithet scrawled on it. They decided it was time to move away.

They moved their six birth children and four adopted children to a rural farmhouse northwest of the city. There, too, they encountered prejudice. At the time, they were caring for a girl with a very low IQ. She was hard to control and had a tendency to run around in their new church. Because of her behavior, they were asked not to bring her back. They knew they could no longer attend that church. When their older children asked why, they could only tell them that even people in church have problems, and believing in God does not make you perfect.

Despite these and similar difficulties, Patty says she wishes she could give the children she is raising today the same sense of community her family enjoyed in their old neighborhood. She recalls a time when one of their young children was molested on her way to school. The policeman who came to the house to investigate lived in the neighborhood. In those days, no one received professional counseling, but that evening, everyone who lived in the neighborhood assembled in front of their house to express their support.

Patty was able to say to her daughter, "Look at all our friends. You know we are going to be all right." Every day for the rest of the school year, when children were traveling to or from school, there was a parent on every street corner in the neighborhood. Patty remembers fondly how everyone knew everyone else. She laments that kids today do not know their neighbors the way people did then.

Patty and Ron say that taking on children with disabilities was not part of their plan. Had they not adopted a disabled child by accident, they probably would never have done so. Says Patty: "We just didn't have it in us." Once they adopted their first child and dropped the idea of adopting Vietnamese children, word got out that they could provide a good home to children in need.

Soon thereafter, Patty and Ron began to be bombarded by requests to take on additional children. Patty says she wishes every person who enjoys being a parent would consider adopting one child, because there are so many in need. The range of their abilities and disabilities is so great that most people would not need to take on a child with disabilities anywhere near as severe as David's.

Each year Patty and Ron continued accepting children, they said it would be their last. They planned to start providing strictly foster care, keeping children only until a good home could be found for them. Over the years, they served as foster parents for dozens of children.

At the time Patty and Ron stopped adopting, they had a total of six foster children in their home. One of the foster children was a ten-year-old boy with cerebral palsy. After some time, an adoptive home was found. He would be adopted by a single mother who had been counseled about the extra demands of caring for a handicapped child. About two months after she took the boy into her home, however, she realized he was too much for her. The boy came back to Patty and Ron. Patty was always distraught over what would happen to their six foster children.

One day soon thereafter, Ron telephoned the caseworker and told her they were going to adopt all those children. He called an attorney to start adoption proceedings. Then he called Patty and told her, "You can quit your crying, because they are ours." She was relieved and overjoyed.

At that point, Patty and Ron closed their home. They had adopted a total of fifteen children. With their six birth children, this brought the total number of their children to twenty-one. One of the last six children they adopted was David.

When some of us encounter a child with severe disabilities, we see only a misshapen human being with whom we have no desire to interact. One disabled child in a wheelchair, just like a beggar on the street, looks much the same as any other. To parents, however, such children seem as distinct from one another as members of our own family. What some of us see as just another defective child seems to them a very special person. Where some of us see only deformed features and stunted abilities, others see a human being who inspires not only love but pride.

David's life looks very different to his brothers and sisters than it would to most people. Most of us would see David as a very sick young man whose life is likely to draw to a close very soon. David's siblings have been told many times that his end was drawing near, and they have developed a different attitude toward life and death. They do not see him as someone who is dying. They see him as someone who will live a long time.

To David's brothers and sisters, his life is not so impoverished that they unconsciously wish for it to end as soon as possible. They do not wish for his death as a relief or release. Instead, they see David's life as fundamentally good. They sincerely believe that his presence enriches their lives. If David were to die, they would grieve. They would miss him.

Spending time with David provides an extraordinary glimpse into the innocence and capacity for loving acceptance of small children. One of David's nephews likes to hold David's foot when he receives his medicines. He stands at David's side, taking his foot in his hand, and patiently strokes it until all the medicines have been given. When it is finished, he lets go and returns to what he was doing.

While the little boy might never say so, it is clear that he thinks he is comforting David. He does not like to take medicines, and he naturally assumes that David doesn't either. He sees David not as an uncle in the usual sense, but as a baby, even though David is quite a bit bigger than he is. David cannot talk or walk or do the other things he can do. Seeing David as a baby, he naturally does what anyone would do with a baby. He supports and comforts him.

David has another young nephew who likes to shake hands. Whenever he sees another male, he shakes his hand. David, of course, cannot shake hands. So when David's nephew is visiting, Ron takes David's hand in his own and shakes it for him. For whom does he do this? Is it for David's nephew? Is it for David?

This is hard to say. The little boy certainly takes pleasure in the fact that David shakes his hand. It simply never occurs to him that David is someone whose hand he need not shake. To him, David is not so severely disabled that he does not count as a person. Instead, he sees David as one of the men and boys to whom it is appropriate to extend the hand of greeting.

One of David's nieces practices a similar ritual. When she arrives at her grandparents' house, she first kisses and hugs both of her grandparents. Then she runs through the house, bursts into David's bedroom, jumps up onto his bed, and gives him a big kiss and hug. She then lies down next to him and talks with him. As she has gotten older, she recently altered this pattern slightly. Now she lies down on her back next to him and reads him a book.

David's niece does not regard him as a pathetic creature for whom she has a duty to care. She is not forcing herself to forget that David cannot understand what she is reading. She is simply sharing with him one of the best things she has to offer; namely, her newly developed ability to read.

Perhaps some day she will no longer burst into David's room and jump up onto his bed. Perhaps some day she will cease to read to him. However, she will always rejoice at the opportunity to see him, and when she does, she will always give him a hug and kiss. To her grandmother, one thing seems certain: No matter how old she is, she will always carry a piece of David in her heart.

22

ETHICS AND METAPHYSICS

Ultimately, our understanding of generosity reflects our understanding of the world we inhabit. If we think the world is a harsh, stingy, and unforgiving place, then we are likely to find ourselves operating from a mentality of scarcity. Those of us whose biological worldview is grounded in winner-take-all competition see the events around us as manifestations of that strife. If we think life is all about seeing that people get what they deserve, then the idea of justice naturally dominates our moral horizon. In each case, ethics grows out of metaphysics. Our sense of how things ought to go grows out of our sense of how the world is. Before we decide what kind of life to lead, we discover what kind of place we inhabit. When we inquire into our vision of the good life, we uncover tacit convictions about reality itself.

What if, for example, the most fundamental force in the universe is not justice or competition or even the second law of thermodynamics, which says that things tend to fall apart? What if the most fundamental force in the universe is not strife or chaos, but love? The Bible teaches that the world exists not because God owed anything to any of his prospective creatures, or even out of metaphysical necessity, but rather from grace. It exists because of an overflowing of divine goodness, a superabundance of love that expresses itself in the very fabric of reality. It is not a fundamentally evil, strife-ridden, or even lonely place, but rather a place filled with possibilities for sharing. Its contents and resources are not meant to be hoarded by its inhabitants, but shared, as their source shares them with us.

When we think about our place in the universe, we seem infinitesimally small. The height of a human being is about one ten millionth of the diameter of the earth. The diameter of the earth, in turn, is about one ten thousandth of the distance from the earth to the sun. This distance is only about one millionth of the distance between our sun and the nearest star. And the distance between the sun and the nearest star is about one twenty-five thousandth of the diameter of the galaxy, which in turn is about one two-hundred thousandth of the size of the known universe. The mass of a human being is measured in tens of kilograms, while the mass of the earth is measured in tens of kilograms to the twenty-fourth power (multiplying ten by ten twenty-four times), and the mass of the sun is tens of kilograms to the thirtieth power.

In other words, any human being, in fact all human beings, are unimaginably small parts of an unimaginably large whole. That we are small, however, does not mean that we are necessarily unimportant. What we lack quantitatively in bulk we make up for qualitatively in special powers that these massive objects lack. These are our powers to know and love. Although the earth and the sun are bigger by an incredible margin than a human being, neither one, so far as we know, is aware of itself. We can do things they cannot. We can calculate the diameter and mass of the earth and sun. We can study the composition of the sun and the earth's inhabitants. Some of these inhabitants we can not only know but love. These are activities of which the vast majority of objects in the universe seem to be utterly incapable.

We too are made up of matter, but we are a special kind of matter. We are matter aware of itself, concerned with itself, and engaged in relationships of a sort that mere physical forces such as electromagnetism and gravity do not begin to capture. In a universe made up mainly of matter in motion, we are something special. All living things have powers that inanimate matter lacks, such as growth, development, reproduction, and metabolism, the ability to sustain our existence by taking in matter and energy from the world around us. The sun is merely burning up its fuel, but a living organism uses food to recreate itself. Compared to plants, animals have still more powers, such as the ability to sense and respond to the environment, and to move about on their own power. To be an animal is to desire, to be turned outward toward the world around us.

Just as plants differ qualitatively from inanimate matter and animals differ qualitatively from plants, so human beings seem to differ qualitatively from other animals. We differ in our special powers to know and to love. In comparison with the creatures of fantasy, we may seem limited. Unlike the Greek gods or contemporary comic book heroes, we are not immortal or invulnerable. We are incapable of unaided flight, lack X-ray vision and the ability to render ourselves invisible, and cannot lift objects that weigh significantly more than we do. However, we do possess these remarkable capacities to know and love. We are not the universe, the galaxy, the sun, the earth, the sky, the ocean, a tree, or a squirrel, and yet we are capable of understanding each of them. From the starry universe above to the smallest subatomic particles of which all matter is made, as well as the forces governing interactions at each of these levels, our minds range over a great expanse of creation.

What if, compared to other creatures, we have been given super powers? What if we are the creatures endowed with the capacity not only to exist, but to know and love one another as well? What if each of us has such super powers but we tend not to notice them because every one else has them too? What if our failure to notice them means that these powers often go largely untapped? What if most of us go through life without realizing our full potential? What if, compared to other creatures, we are like angels, capable of participating to some degree in the divine through these powers to know and love? What if our curiosity is a gateway to richer dimensions of reality? What if our capacity to love is an invitation to glimpse the mind of God?

Such a vision may appear fanciful, but what if it is true? If we viewed ourselves from such a perspective, what would we look like? To what or to whom would we see ourselves as responsible? What would we see ourselves as living for? This is not to suggest that we carry the weight of the world, the care of the entire universe, on our shoulders. It does suggest that the choices we make about our time and attention may be weightier than we ordinarily suppose. What if, for example, not only our generically human abilities to know and love but even our distinctive individual interests and talents are powers that we are meant to make the most of? What if we are not so much the possessors of our abilities as their stewards, carrying around within ourselves resources whose potential we have yet to fully realize?

What would this say about giving and sharing, and the possibilities for excellence in each of us? Among other things, it might say that we should be on the lookout for possibilities. Perhaps part of our mission in life is not merely to give what we have to people in need, but to draw out from the world and the people around us goodness that would otherwise remain invisible. In the Genesis account, God says, "Let there be light," human beings are said to be made in God's image, and God inspects his handiwork and pronounces it good. What if our mission is a semidivine one—to bring goodness to light? Even if we are not the light's source, we can still act as lenses, refracting and focusing the light on otherwise hidden things. Perhaps this is what Jesus intended in calling human beings the light of the world.

Approaching giving and sharing from this point of view, we might not be surprised to discover that new opportunities for generosity continually emerge in the course of our lives. It is not just that we cannot foresee all our opportunities to give, but that what we expect to give is not what someone else wants or needs. To give well, we must be prepared to take our cues from others, to learn from them. This is not a philanthropy of imposition, in which we impose our views on those we judge to be in need. It is a philanthropy of collaboration, in which we work together to enrich the lives of both givers and receivers. Such generosity is not like a drill sergeant barking out orders to the troops, but like two people dancing. One may lead and the other may follow, but both are constantly adjusting to one another.

Our most important philanthropic resource is not money. It is not even our time or our talent. Our most important philanthropic resource is our imagination, our dreams. What do we think is possible? What purposes larger than ourselves are we capable of discerning and working on behalf of? In some respects, we are the instruments of those purposes. Yet it is truer to say that we collaborate actively with them. When we recognize dreams as our most important philanthropic resource, we realize that one of the greatest gifts we can give another person is to believe in them, even when they don't believe in themselves. This can be as complex as devoting part of our lives to them, and as simple as giving them our undivided attention. When we do that, we transform our narrative perspective from, "What is my story?" to "What story are we in?"

What story are we in? Is it a story of disappointment and frustration? Or is it a story of abundance and gratitude? To a large extent, the answer to these questions hinges on our own sense of resourcefulness. If we feel we are always laboring under conditions of scarcity, in which we do not have enough to do and be what is needed, then disappointment will dominate. Those who feel that reality itself is too stingy, or that they never get enough from others, tend to believe that other people are insensitive, or even cruel. Their attitude toward others is, "Give them a chance, and they will take everything they can get." They have no interest in giving. At their worst, such people may lapse into cynicism toward others, finding selfishness and fear in even the most generous of acts. They know the cost of everything, but the value of nothing.

The cynic's problem is not hatred, but fear. When we fear other people, we naturally tend to avoid getting involved with them. We have no interest in investing ourselves in their lives, and instead seek to distance ourselves from them. We think we cannot bear them, that mixing just a little of their perspective into our lives will ruin us. At its core, cynicism is a form of cowardice.

How can we move beyond it? By recognizing that we draw from a deeper well than we suppose. Putting a pinch of salt in a drop of water makes it offensive to the taste, but if we dissolve that same pinch of salt in a large pool, its effect is minimal. Our ability to bear the sufferings of others hinges not only on the magnitude of their afflictions, but also on the depth of our own resources. If we develop ourselves fully, how much could we really contain?

If we view others' suffering with compassion, which is to say courageously, even our failures turn out to be less terrible than we suppose. If the container cracks, it can still be mended. Sometimes, in fact, it is the fissures that turn out to be most revealing. The cracks let in the light, helping us to understand the full extent of our own limitations and illuminating the true nature of the resources we have at our disposal. Suppose that instead of keeping a stiff upper lip, our firm and reassuring countenance begins to melt, and we break down in tears. Have we failed those we are seeking to help? In some cases, those tears may be the greatest testament, the greatest comfort and support, we can offer. They show that we really care, that we are able to let down our guard and admit that we too are human and do not have all the answers.

To love is to admit our vulnerability. When we fall in love with someone, such as a newborn child, we open up a new place in our heart. Everything that happens to that child also happens to us. When the child suffers, we suffer, and as any parent will attest, that vulnerability does not vanish as the child migrates from childhood to adulthood. Our sense of well-being and happiness is always bound up with those we love. The human mission is not to make ourselves as invulnerable as possible, to shield ourselves in an impenetrable fortress, but to keep the gates open. When we sense the full extent and value of what we have, not materially, but psychologically and spiritually, then keeping the gates open ceases to seem a duty and becomes instead an opportunity. Life is simply more engaging, every day richer and more profound, when we live compassionately.

Love changes everything. The same situation can look quite different depending on whether or not we approach it with love. From the vantage point of fear and cynicism, we see only shadows, specters. Their very presence makes us jittery, prone to withdraw or lash out at the first sign of trouble. When we approach others with love, however, we reveal the extraordinary in the ordinary and open up new dimensions of meaning that would otherwise remain sealed off from us. What might first seem an intrusion on our time or a threat to our psychological equilibrium becomes one of our deepest and most fulfilling experiences, a genuinely human encounter that we carry with us for the rest of our lives. In seeing others with love, we see who they really are. In seeing others with love, we see who we really are.

To be sure, our resources are finite. No one is truly tireless, blessed with unbounded energy. Even the greatest healers and prophets needed time to eat and sleep. Jesus Christ sometimes withdrew from crowds and his disciples even though there were people who needed him. The point of sounding the true depths of our resources is not to say that our supply is limitless, but to point out that most of us seriously underestimate what we are capable of. That the supply is finite does not mean we should hoard as much as we can until the last possible moment. It means we should recognize the renewability of our resources, which like muscles and minds grow stronger as we put them to use. Whatever the limit of our energy, our challenge is to develop and direct it as fruitfully as we can. We simply cannot afford to squander it in fear.

When we share lovingly the best we have to offer, we realize that we are not denying ourselves, but fulfilling ourselves. We are not depleting ourselves, but enriching ourselves. Until we give lovingly, we are but prisoners of our own fears and misapprehensions. At first, it is a shock to realize that we can part with something, even the things we think we hold most dear, without feeling that a part of us has been amputated. We are not like machines losing parts. We are like trees sending out roots, or better yet, casting their seeds to the wind. Take the example of a book. When we give a great book as a gift, we do not diminish its value. We increase it. In sharing it with others, we increase the contribution it makes to their lives. We give even more when we allow it to spawn a conversation. A book moldering unread on a shelf is like a gift never given, its potential unrealized.

Good books and the conversations they spawn help us recover our identity. They draw us back to the things we need to be reminded of. They help us remember the many people who came before us and turn our imaginations to those who will come after us. When we read and discuss them with care, good books help us appreciate that our traditions are not constraining, but rather empowering and even liberating. We are capable of contributing much more when we see ourselves in the company of those who depend on us to make the most of what we have been given. Their words are with us in such books. Perhaps they are right here beside us now, challenging us to look more deeply and filling us with the courage we need to be true to what we find. "Give," they are saying. "Go ahead and give!"

SUGGESTED READINGS

Addams, Jane, et al. *Philanthropy and Social Progress; Seven Essays.* New York: Crowell, 1893.

Anderson, Charles W. *A Deeper Freedom: Liberal Democracy as an Everyday Morality.* Madison: University of Wisconsin Press, 2002.

Aristotle. *Nicomachean Ethics* (2nd ed.). Indianapolis, Ind.: Hackett, 2000.

Aristotle. *Politics.* Indianapolis, Ind.: Hackett, 1998.

Babbitt, Susan E. *Artless Integrity: Moral Imagination, Agency, and Stories.* Lanham, Md.: Rowman & Littlefield, 2001.

Bangert, Byron C. *Moral Issues and Motivations in Medical Philanthropy.* Bloomington, Ind.: Poynter Center for the Study of Ethics and American Institutions, Indiana University, 2005.

Banner, Michael C. *Christian Ethics and Contemporary Moral Problems.* New York: Cambridge University Press, 1999.

Barber, Nigel. *Kindness in a Cruel World: The Evolution of Altruism.* Amherst, N.Y.: Prometheus Books, 2004.

Bell, Daniel. *Communitarianism and its Critics.* Oxford: Clarendon, 1993.

Bok, Sissela. *Common Values.* Columbia: University of Missouri Press, 1995.

Broome, John. *Weighing Lives.* Oxford: Oxford University Press, 2006.

Carnegie, Andrew. *The Gospel of Wealth.* Carlisle, Mass.: Applewood Books, 1998.

Cervantes, Miguel de. *Don Quixote.* London: Harper Perennial, 2005.

Charvet, John. *The Idea of an Ethical Community.* Ithaca, N.Y.: Cornell University Press, 1995.

Coffin, William Sloane. *The Heart Is a Little to the Left: Essays on Public Morality.* Hanover, N.H.: University Press of New England [for] Dartmouth College, 1999.

Crisp, Roger, ed. *How Should One Live? Essays on the Virtues.* Oxford: Clarendon; New York: Oxford University Press, 1998.

Cunningham, Anthony. *The Heart of What Matters: The Role for Literature in Moral Philosophy.* Berkeley: University of California Press, 2001.

Dante. *Divine Comedy.* New York: Everyman's Library, 1995.

Denham, A. E. *Metaphor and Moral Experience.* Oxford: Clarendon; New York: Oxford University Press, 2000.

Dickens, Charles. *A Christmas Carol.* Clayton, Del.: Prestwick House, 2005.

Dostoyevsky, Fyodor. *The Brothers Karamazov.* New York: MacMillan, 1995.

Driver, Julia. *Uneasy Virtue.* Cambridge; New York: Cambridge University Press, 2001.

Eberly, Don E. *The Soul of Civil Society: Voluntary Associations and the Public Value of Moral Habits.* Lanham, Md.: Lexington Books, 2002.

Edwards, Jonathan. *The Nature of True Virtue.* Ann Arbor: University of Michigan Press, 1996.

Eliot, George. *Middlemarch.* New York: Signet Classics (reissue edition), 2003.

Elliott, Deni. *The Kindness of Strangers: Philanthropy and Higher Education.* Lanham, Md.: Rowman & Littlefield, 2006.

Erikson, Erik. *The Golden Rule in the Light of New Insight. The Erik Erikson Reader.* Edited by Robert Coles. New York: Norton, 2001.

Etzioni, Amitai, Andrew Volmert, and Elanit Rothschild, eds. *The Communitarian Reader: Beyond the Essentials.* Lanham, Md.: Rowman & Littlefield, 2004.

Fleishman, Joel. *The Foundation: A Great American Secret.* New York: Public Affairs, 2007.

Frumkin, Peter. *Strategic Giving.* Chicago: University of Chicago Press, 2006.

Gaita, Raimond. *A Common Humanity: Thinking about Love and Truth and Justice.* New York: Routledge, 2002.

Gilman, James Earl. *Fidelity of Heart: An Ethic of Christian Virtue.* Oxford: Oxford University Press, 2001.

Grene, David, and Richard Lattimore. *The Complete Greek Tragedies.* Chicago: University of Chicago Press, 1991.

Gustafson, James. *Ethics from a Theocentric Perspective,* Volume I. Chicago: University of Chicago Press, 1983.

Haughey, John C. *Virtue and Affluence: The Challenge of Wealth.* Kansas City, Mo.: Sheed & Ward, 1997.

Hippocrates. *The Hippocratic Oath.*

Hobbes, Thomas. *Leviathan.* New York: Penguin Classics, 1982.

Homer. *The Odyssey.* Translated by Robert Fagles. New York: Penguin Classics (reissue edition), 2006.

Hooker, Brad, and Margaret Olivia Little, eds. *Moral Particularism.* Oxford: Clarendon Press; New York: Oxford University Press, 2000.

Kant, Immanuel. *The Metaphysics of Morals.* Cambridge; New York: Cambridge University Press, 1991.

Kass, Amy. *The Perfect Gift: The Philanthropic Imagination in Poetry and Prose.* Bloomington: Indiana University Press, 2002.

Kass, Leon. *The Beginning of Wisdom: Reading Genesis.* Chicago: University of Chicago Press, 2006.

Katakis, Michael, ed. *Sacred Trusts: Essays on Stewardship and Responsibility.* San Francisco: Mercury House, 1993.

Kirkpatrick, Frank G. *The Ethics of Community.* Malden, Mass.: Blackwell, 2001.

Lao-Tse. *Te-Tao Ching.* New York: Ballantine Books, 1992.

Lear, Jonathan. *Aristotle: The Desire to Understand.* Cambridge: Cambridge University Press, 1988.

Machiavelli, Niccolò. *The Prince.* New York: Bantam Classics, 1984.

Marty, Martin E. *Being Good and Doing Good.* Philadelphia: Fortress, 1984.

May, William F., and A. Lewis Soens, Jr., eds. *The Ethics of Giving and Receiving: Am I My Foolish Brother's Keeper?* Dallas, Tex.: Cary M. Maguire Center for Ethics and Public Responsibility, Southern Methodist University Press, 2000.

McCourt, Frank. *Angela's Ashes.* London: Harper Perennial (new edition), 2005.

McDowell, Banks. *Ethics and Excuses: The Crisis in Professional Responsibility.* Westport, Conn.: Quorum Books, 2000.

Mill, John Stuart. *On Liberty.* New York: Penguin Classics (new edition), 1982.

Molière, Jean-Baptiste. *The Miser and Other Plays.* New York: Penguin Classics, 1953.

Myers, David G. *The American Paradox: Spiritual Hunger in an Age of Plenty.* New Haven, Conn.: Yale University Press, 2000.

Neusner, Jacob, and Noam M. M. Neusner, eds. *The Book of Jewish Wisdom: The Talmud of the Well-Considered Life.* New York: Continuum, 1996.

New English Bible. Oxford and Cambridge: Oxford University Press and Cambridge University Press, 1961.

Obedience to the Unenforceable: Ethics and the Nation's Voluntary and Philanthropic Community. Washington, D.C.: Independent Sector, 2002.

Payton, Robert. *Philanthropy: Voluntary Action for the Public Good.* Westport, Conn.: Oryx Press, 1988.

Plato. *Meno.* Indianapolis, Ind.: Hackett (2nd ed.), 1976.

———. *The Republic.* New York: Penguin Classics (2nd ed.), 2003.

Pojman, Louis P., ed. *Life and Death: A Reader in Moral Problems*. Belmont, Calif.: Wadsworth Pub. Co., 2000.

Rand, Ayn. *The Virtue of Selfishness*. New York: Signet (reissue edition), 1964.

Reis, Burkhard, and Stella Haffmans, eds. *The Virtuous Life in Greek Ethics*. Cambridge; New York: Cambridge University Press, 2006.

Rossi, Alice, ed. *Caring and Doing for Others: Social Responsibility in the Domains of Family, Work, and Community*. Chicago: University of Chicago Press, 2001.

Schervish, Paul G. *The Study on Wealth and Philanthropy: Final Report*. Chestnut Hill, Mass.: Social Welfare Research Institute, Boston College, 1988.

Schweiker, William. *Responsibility and Christian Ethics*. Cambridge; New York: Cambridge University Press, 1995.

Shakespeare, William. *King Lear*. Oxford: Arden (3rd ed.), 1997.

Sims, Ronald R. *Ethics and Corporate Social Responsibility: Why Giants Fall*. Westport, Conn.: Praeger, 2003.

Smith, Adam. *The Theory of Moral Sentiments*. Whitefish, Mont.: Kessinger Publishing, 2004.

Smith, David H., ed. *Good Intentions: Moral Obstacles and Opportunities*. Bloomington: Indiana University Press, 2005.

Steinbeck, John. *The Grapes of Wrath*. New York: Penguin (Non-Classics), 1991.

Tamari, Meir. *The Challenge of Wealth: A Jewish Perspective on Earning and Spending Money*. Northvale, N.J.: J. Aronson, 1995.

Tolstoy, Leo. *Great Short Works of Leo Tolstoy*. New York: Harper Perennial Modern Classics (reprint edition), 2004.

Troeltsch, Ernst. *The Social Teaching of the Christian Churches*. Louisville, Ky.: Westminster/John Knox Press, 1992.

Vogel, David. *The Market for Virtue: The Potential and Limits of Corporate Social Responsibility*. Washington, D.C.: Brookings Institution Press, 2005.

Walzer, Michael. *On Toleration*. New Haven, Conn.: Yale University Press, 1997.

Wheeler, Sondra Ely. *Wealth as Peril and Obligation: The New Testament on Possessions*. Grand Rapids, Mich.: W. B. Eerdmans Pub., 1995.

White, Stephen A. *Sovereign Virtue: Aristotle on the Relation between Happiness and Prosperity*. Stanford, Calif.: Stanford University Press, 2007.

Williams, Oliver F., ed. *The Moral Imagination: How Literature and Films Can Stimulate Ethical Reflection in the Business World*. Notre Dame, Ind.: University of Notre Dame Press, 1997.

RICHARD B. GUNDERMAN is vice chairman, radiology; director, pediatric radiology; and associate professor of radiology, pediatrics, medical education, philosophy, liberal arts, and philanthropy at Indiana University–Purdue University at Indianapolis (IUPUI).